SAFe® Scrum Master

Exam Companion :

Q & A with Explanations

SUJAN

SAFe® Scrum Master

Exam Companion

:Q & A with Explanations

FIRST EDITION. September 20th, 2024.

COPYRIGHT © 2024 SUJAN.

Written by SUJAN

CONTENTS

(Multiple-Choice Questions with Detailed
Explanations)

Introduction

Welcome to "SAFe Scrum Master Exam Companion: Q&A with Explanations", your ultimate resource for achieving excellence in the SAFe Scrum Master (SSM) certification exam. This comprehensive guide is designed to be your trusted companion on the journey to mastering SAFe principles, Scrum frameworks, and Agile methodologies.

In today's complex and rapidly changing business landscape, the SAFe Scrum Master certification is a highly valued credential that validates your expertise in scaling Agile practices across the enterprise. This book is meticulously crafted to provide you with the knowledge, confidence, and practical insights needed to excel in the exam and thrive as a SAFe Scrum Master.

Through a unique Q&A format paired with detailed explanations, "SAFe Scrum Master Exam Companion" delves into the core concepts of SAFe, Scrum, and Agile methodologies, immersing you in real-world scenarios and applications. With 315 expertly crafted questions and 7 practice exams mirroring the actual exam experience, this guide is tailored to deepen your understanding and equip you with the tools to succeed.

Whether you're new to SAFe or seeking to reinforce your existing expertise, this companion guide will help you:

- Master SAFe principles, values, and practices
- Understand Scrum frameworks and Agile methodologies
- Develop practical skills in Iteration Planning, Product Backlog management, and team facilitation

- Analyze complex scenarios and apply SAFe principles to real-world challenges

Embark on a transformative journey of self-discovery and growth as you explore SAFe, Scrum, and Agile concepts. With its comprehensive coverage and practical insights, "SAFe Scrum Master Exam Companion" empowers you to unlock a world of Agile possibilities and achieve your SAFe Scrum Master certification goals.

Are you ready to elevate your SAFe knowledge and skills? Let this companion guide be your trusted ally on the path to SAFe Scrum Master success.

Key Features:

- 315 expertly crafted questions with detailed explanations
- 7 practice exams simulating the actual exam experience
- Comprehensive coverage of SAFe principles, Scrum frameworks, and Agile methodologies
- Real-world scenarios and applications
- Practical insights and expert guidance

Get ready to pass the SAFe Scrum Master exam with confidence!

PRACTICE TEST - 1

Question 1

What is the primary goal of the Innovation and Planning (IP) Iteration in SAFe?

A) To prioritize and refine the Program Backlog

B) To develop and deliver working software

C) To plan and prepare for the next Program Increment

D) To innovate, experiment, and plan for the future

Answer: D) To innovate, experiment, and plan for the future

Explanation: The IP Iteration is a dedicated iteration in SAFe that allows teams to innovate, experiment, and plan for the future. It provides a buffer for unexpected work and allows teams to prepare for the next Program Increment.

Question 2

Which of the following is a key responsibility of a Scrum Master in SAFe?

A) Prioritizing the Program Backlog

B) Coordinating dependencies between teams

C) Facilitating Scrum events and removing impediments

D) Managing and allocating team resources

Answer: C) Facilitating Scrum events and removing impediments

Explanation: The Scrum Master is responsible for facilitating Scrum events, such as Sprint Planning, Daily Scrum, Sprint Review, and Sprint Retrospective. They also work to remove impediments that obstruct the team's progress and foster an environment of continuous improvement.

Question 3

In SAFe, what is the purpose of the Program Kanban?

A) To visualize the flow of work across teams

B) To prioritize the Program Backlog

C) To manage dependencies between teams

D) To track progress towards Program Increment goals

Answer: A) To visualize the flow of work across teams

Explanation: The Program Kanban is a visualization tool that shows the flow of work across teams, allowing teams to manage the flow of work, identify bottlenecks, and improve delivery.

Question 4

Which of the following is a key characteristic of a High-Performing Team in SAFe?

A) Team members have specialized roles and responsibilities

B) Team members are collocated and work on a single feature

C) Team members are cross-functional and self-organizing

D) Team members work independently with minimal collaboration

Answer: C) Team members are cross-functional and self-organizing

Explanation: High-Performing Teams in SAFe are characterized by being cross-functional, meaning they have the skills and expertise to deliver a feature or component without dependencies on others. They are also self-organizing, meaning they take ownership and make decisions about their work.

QUESTION 5

In SAFe, what is the purpose of the Solution Demo?

A) To showcase the work of a single Agile Team

B) To demonstrate the integration of solutions across teams

C) To prioritize the Program Backlog

D) To track progress towards Program Increment goals

Answer: B) To demonstrate the integration of solutions across teams

Explanation: The Solution Demo is an event where the work of multiple Agile Teams is integrated and demonstrated to stakeholders, providing a broader view of the solution and its progress.

Question 6

Which of the following is a key aspect of the SAFe Lean-Agile Mindset?

A) Focus on individual team performance

B) Emphasis on predicting and controlling outcomes

C) Encouragement of experimentation and learning

D) Prioritization of efficiency over effectiveness

Answer: C) Encouragement of experimentation and learning

Explanation: The SAFe Lean-Agile Mindset emphasizes the importance of experimentation, learning, and continuous improvement, encouraging teams to take calculated risks and learn from their experiences.

Question 7

In SAFe, what is the role of the Release Train Engineer (RTE) in facilitating the Program Increment (PI) Planning event?

A) To prioritize the Program Backlog

B) To facilitate the team breakout sessions

C) To manage the program's budget and resources

D) To ensure the program's alignment with the company's strategy

Answer: B) To facilitate the team breakout sessions

Explanation: The Release Train Engineer (RTE) plays a key role in facilitating the PI Planning event, specifically in guiding the team breakout sessions to ensure that teams are aligned and have a clear understanding of their objectives and dependencies.

Question 8

Which of the following is a benefit of using the Built-In Quality practices in SAFe?

A) Reduced testing and validation efforts

B) Improved predictability and reduced variability

C) Increased efficiency through automation

D) Enhanced collaboration and communication among teams

Answer: B) Improved predictability and reduced variability

Explanation: Built-In Quality practices in SAFe aim to ensure that quality is integrated into every aspect of the development process, resulting in improved predictability and reduced variability in the delivery of working software.

Question 9

In SAFe, what is the primary purpose of the Program Board?

A) To visualize the Program Backlog

B) To track the progress of individual teams

C) To manage dependencies and flow across teams

D) To prioritize features for the next Program Increment

Answer: C) To manage dependencies and flow across teams

Explanation: The Program Board is a visualization tool that helps teams manage dependencies and flow across teams, enabling them to identify and address potential bottlenecks and improve the overall delivery of the program.

Question 10

Which of the following is a key aspect of the SAFe Continuous Delivery Pipeline?

A) Manual testing and validation

B) Automated testing and continuous integration

C) Separate development and operations teams

D) Focus on releasing software to production infrequently

Answer: B) Automated testing and continuous integration

Explanation: The SAFe Continuous Delivery Pipeline emphasizes automated testing and continuous integration to ensure that code changes are quickly and reliably delivered to production, reducing the time and effort required to release new features and improvements.

Question 11

In SAFe, what is the role of the System Architect in the Agile Release Train (ART)?

A) To define and manage the Program Backlog

B) To ensure the technical integrity of the system

C) To coordinate the work of multiple Agile Teams

D) To prioritize features for the next Program Increment

Answer: B) To ensure the technical integrity of the system

Explanation: The System Architect plays a critical role in ensuring the technical integrity of the system, making strategic technical decisions, and providing technical guidance to Agile Teams.

Question 12

Which of the following is a key benefit of implementing SAFe's Lean Portfolio Management (LPM)?

A) Improved resource utilization and allocation

B) Enhanced predictability and reduced variability

C) Increased agility and responsiveness to change

D) All of the above

Answer: D) All of the above

Explanation: Lean Portfolio Management (LPM) in SAFe provides several benefits, including improved resource utilization and allocation, enhanced predictability and reduced variability, and increased agility and responsiveness to change, enabling organizations to deliver value more efficiently and effectively.

Question 13

In SAFe, what is the purpose of the Inspect and Adapt (I&A) event?

A) To plan the next Program Increment

B) To demonstrate the work of the Agile Teams

C) To reflect on and improve the Agile Release Train's processes

D) To prioritize the Program Backlog

Answer: C) To reflect on and improve the Agile Release Train's processes

Explanation: The Inspect and Adapt (I&A) event is a critical event in SAFe that allows the Agile Release Train (ART) to reflect on its processes, identify areas for improvement, and implement changes to increase efficiency and effectiveness.

Question 14

Which of the following is a key characteristic of a SAFe Agile Team?

A) Team members have specialized roles and responsibilities

B) Team members are collocated and work on a single feature

C) Team members are cross-functional and self-organizing

D) Team members work independently with minimal collaboration

Answer: C) Team members are cross-functional and self-organizing

Explanation: SAFe Agile Teams are characterized by being cross-functional, meaning they have the skills and expertise to deliver a feature or component without dependencies on others, and self-organizing, meaning they take ownership and make decisions about their work.

Question 15

In SAFe, what is the role of the Business Owners in the Agile Release Train (ART)?

A) To prioritize the Program Backlog

B) To provide input on business requirements and value

C) To manage the budget and resources for the ART

D) To ensure compliance with regulatory requirements

Answer: B) To provide input on business requirements and value

Explanation: Business Owners play a crucial role in SAFe by providing input on business requirements and value, ensuring that the ART delivers solutions that meet business needs and provide value to customers.

Question 16

Which of the following is a key aspect of SAFe's DevOps and Continuous Delivery Pipeline?

A) Manual testing and validation

B) Automated testing and continuous integration

C) Separate development and operations teams

D) Focus on releasing software to production infrequently

Answer: B) Automated testing and continuous integration

Explanation: SAFe's DevOps and Continuous Delivery Pipeline emphasizes automated testing and continuous integration to ensure that code changes are quickly and reliably delivered to production, reducing the time and effort required to release new features and improvements.

Question 17

In SAFe, what is the purpose of the Program Increment (PI) Objectives?

A) To define the scope of the Program Backlog

B) To establish the budget for the Agile Release Train

C) To provide a shared understanding of the program's goals

D) To prioritize features for the next PI

Answer: C) To provide a shared understanding of the program's goals

Explanation: PI Objectives provide a shared understanding of the program's goals, ensuring that all teams and stakeholders are aligned and working towards the same objectives.

Question 18

Which of the following is a key benefit of implementing SAFe's Lean-Agile Principles?

A) Improved predictability and reduced variability

B) Enhanced collaboration and communication among teams

C) Increased efficiency through automation

D) All of the above

Answer: D) All of the above

Explanation: Implementing SAFe's Lean-Agile Principles provides several benefits, including improved predictability and reduced variability, enhanced collaboration and communication among teams, and increased efficiency through automation, enabling organizations to deliver value more efficiently and effectively.

Question 19

In SAFe, what is the role of the Scrum Master in facilitating the Program Kanban?

A) To prioritize the Program Backlog

B) To manage the flow of work across teams

C) To facilitate the Scrum events for individual teams

D) To ensure the Program Kanban is up-to-date and accurate

Answer: B) To manage the flow of work across teams

Explanation: The Scrum Master plays a key role in facilitating the Program Kanban by managing the flow of work across teams, ensuring that the program's goals are met, and identifying and addressing bottlenecks and impediments.

Question 20

Which of the following is a key aspect of SAFe's Continuous Learning Culture?

A) Encouraging experimentation and learning from failure

B) Focusing on individual performance and accountability

C) Emphasizing predictability and control over adaptability

D) Prioritizing efficiency over effectiveness

Answer: A) Encouraging experimentation and learning from failure

Explanation: SAFe's Continuous Learning Culture emphasizes encouraging experimentation, learning from failure, and continuous improvement, enabling teams to adapt and innovate in a rapidly changing environment.

Question 21

In SAFe, what is the purpose of the Solution Management role?

A) To prioritize the Program Backlog

B) To manage the solution's budget and resources

C) To define and manage the solution's roadmap

D) To ensure the solution meets customer needs

Answer: C) To define and manage the solution's roadmap

Explanation: The Solution Management role is responsible for defining and managing the solution's roadmap, ensuring that the solution aligns with the organization's strategy and meets customer needs.

Question 22

Which of the following is a key benefit of implementing SAFe's Agile Release Trains (ARTs)?

A) Improved collaboration and communication among teams

B) Enhanced predictability and reduced variability

C) Increased efficiency through automation

D) All of the above

Answer: D) All of the above

Explanation: Implementing SAFe's Agile Release Trains (ARTs) provides several benefits, including improved collaboration and communication among teams, enhanced predictability and reduced variability, and increased efficiency through automation, enabling organizations to deliver value more efficiently and effectively.

Question 23

In SAFe, what is the purpose of the Innovation and Planning (IP) Iteration?

A) To plan the next Program Increment

B) To innovate and develop new solutions

C) To reflect on and improve the Agile Release Train's processes

D) To demonstrate the work of the Agile Teams

Answer: B) To innovate and develop new solutions

Explanation: The Innovation and Planning (IP) Iteration is a dedicated iteration for innovation, experimentation, and planning, allowing teams to explore new ideas, develop new solutions, and plan for the next Program Increment.

Question 24

Which of the following is a key aspect of SAFe's Lean Portfolio Management (LPM)?

A) Centralized decision-making and control

B) Decentralized decision-making and empowerment

C) Focus on individual project success over portfolio success

D) Emphasis on predictability over adaptability

Answer: B) Decentralized decision-making and empowerment

Explanation: SAFe's Lean Portfolio Management (LPM) emphasizes decentralized decision-making and empowerment, enabling teams and leaders to make decisions and take ownership of their work, and aligning with the organization's strategy and goals.

Question 25

In SAFe, what is the role of the Release Train Engineer (RTE) in facilitating the Program Kanban?

A) To prioritize the Program Backlog

B) To manage the flow of work across teams

C) To ensure the Program Kanban is up-to-date and accurate

D) To facilitate the Scrum events for individual teams

Answer: B) To manage the flow of work across teams

Explanation: The Release Train Engineer (RTE) plays a key role in facilitating the Program Kanban by managing the flow of work across teams, ensuring that the program's goals are met, and identifying and addressing bottlenecks and impediments.

Question 26

Which of the following is a key benefit of implementing SAFe's DevOps and Continuous Delivery Pipeline?

A) Improved collaboration and communication among teams

B) Enhanced predictability and reduced variability

C) Increased speed and efficiency in delivering value to customers

D) All of the above

Answer: D) All of the above

Explanation: Implementing SAFe's DevOps and Continuous Delivery Pipeline provides several benefits, including improved collaboration and communication among teams, enhanced predictability and reduced variability, and increased speed and efficiency in delivering value to customers, enabling organizations to respond quickly to changing market conditions.

Question 27

In SAFe, what is the purpose of the Guardian of the Brand role?

A) To ensure alignment with the organization's strategy

B) To prioritize the Program Backlog

C) To manage the solution's budget and resources

D) To ensure customer satisfaction with the solution

Answer: A) To ensure alignment with the organization's strategy

Explanation: The Guardian of the Brand role ensures that the solution aligns with the organization's brand, strategy, and values, and that the solution meets customer needs and expectations.

Question 28

Which of the following is a key aspect of SAFe's Lean-Agile Leadership?

A) Command-and-control leadership style

B) Empowering teams to make decisions and take ownership

C) Focus on individual performance over team performance

D) Emphasis on predictability over adaptability

Answer: B) Empowering teams to make decisions and take ownership

Explanation: SAFe's Lean-Agile Leadership emphasizes empowering teams to make decisions and take ownership of their work, enabling them to respond quickly to changing market conditions and deliver value to customers.

Question 29

In SAFe, what is the purpose of the Solution Demo?

A) To demonstrate the work of individual Agile Teams

B) To showcase the solution's progress to stakeholders

C) To prioritize the Program Backlog

D) To manage the solution's budget and resources

Answer: B) To showcase the solution's progress to stakeholders

Explanation: The Solution Demo is a critical event in SAFe that showcases the solution's progress to stakeholders, providing an opportunity for feedback, alignment, and adaptation.

Question 30

Which of the following is a key benefit of implementing SAFe's Lean Portfolio Management (LPM)?

A) Improved resource utilization and allocation

B) Enhanced predictability and reduced variability

C) Increased agility and responsiveness to change

D) All of the above

Answer: D) All of the above

Explanation: Implementing SAFe's Lean Portfolio Management (LPM) provides several benefits, including improved resource utilization and allocation, enhanced predictability and reduced variability, and increased agility and responsiveness to change, enabling organizations to deliver value more efficiently and effectively.

Question 31

In SAFe, what is the role of the Agile Team's Product Owner in the Program Kanban?

A) To prioritize the Program Backlog

B) To manage the flow of work across teams

C) To ensure the team's work aligns with the program's goals

D) To facilitate the Scrum events for the team

Answer: C) To ensure the team's work aligns with the program's goals

Explanation: The Agile Team's Product Owner plays a key role in the Program Kanban by ensuring that the team's work aligns with the program's goals and objectives, and that the team is working on the highest-priority items.

Question 32

Which of the following is a key aspect of SAFe's Continuous Delivery Pipeline?

A) Manual testing and validation

B) Automated testing and continuous integration

C) Separate development and operations teams

D) Focus on releasing software to production infrequently

Answer: B) Automated testing and continuous integration

Explanation: SAFe's Continuous Delivery Pipeline emphasizes automated testing and continuous integration to ensure that code changes are quickly and reliably delivered to production, reducing the time and effort required to release new features and improvements.

Question 33

In SAFe, what is the purpose of the Program Backlog Refinement?

A) To prioritize the Program Backlog

B) To refine and decompose features into user stories

C) To estimate the size and complexity of features

D) To assign work to individual Agile Teams

Answer: B) To refine and decompose features into user stories

Explanation: The Program Backlog Refinement is a critical process in SAFe that involves refining and decomposing features into user stories, ensuring that the work is properly sized and understood by the Agile Teams.

Question 34

Which of the following is a key benefit of implementing SAFe's Lean-Agile Principles?

A) Improved predictability and reduced variability

B) Enhanced collaboration and communication among teams

C) Increased efficiency through automation

D) Ability to manage complex programs with multiple dependencies

Answer: D) Ability to manage complex programs with multiple dependencies

Explanation: Implementing SAFe's Lean-Agile Principles enables organizations to manage complex programs with multiple dependencies, ensuring that the program's goals and objectives are met, and that the work is properly coordinated and aligned.

Question 35

In SAFe, what is the role of the System Architect in the Agile Release Train (ART)?

A) To define the technical vision for the solution

B) To prioritize the Program Backlog

C) To manage the technical debt and architecture runway

D) To ensure compliance with regulatory requirements

Answer: A) To define the technical vision for the solution

Explanation: The System Architect plays a key role in the Agile Release Train (ART) by defining the technical vision for the solution, ensuring that the solution aligns with the organization's technical strategy and architecture.

Question 36

Which of the following is a key aspect of SAFe's Program Increment (PI) Planning?

A) Creating a detailed project plan with timelines and milestones

B) Defining the program's goals and objectives for the next PI

C) Assigning work to individual Agile Teams

D) Estimating the cost and resources required for the next PI

Answer: B) Defining the program's goals and objectives for the next PI

Explanation: SAFe's Program Increment (PI) Planning involves defining the program's goals and objectives for the next PI, ensuring that the program's work aligns with the organization's strategy and goals, and that the Agile Teams are working towards a common objective.

Question 37

In SAFe, what is the purpose of the ART Sync?

A) To synchronize the work of individual Agile Teams

B) To align the program's goals and objectives with the organization's strategy

C) To prioritize the Program Backlog

D) To manage dependencies between Agile Teams

Answer: B) To align the program's goals and objectives with the organization's strategy

Explanation: The ART Sync is a critical event in SAFe that aligns the program's goals and objectives with the organization's strategy, ensuring that the Agile Release Train (ART) is working towards a common objective.

Question 38

Which of the following is a key benefit of implementing SAFe's Continuous Exploration?

A) Improved predictability and reduced variability

B) Enhanced collaboration and communication among teams

C) Increased speed and efficiency in delivering value to customers

D) Ability to explore and validate new ideas and solutions

Answer: D) Ability to explore and validate new ideas and solutions

Explanation: SAFe's Continuous Exploration enables organizations to explore and validate new ideas and solutions, ensuring that the program's work is aligned with customer needs and market trends, and that the organization is innovating and adapting to changing market conditions.

Question 39

In SAFe, what is the role of the Business Owner in the Lean-Agile Enterprise?

A) To prioritize the Program Backlog

B) To ensure alignment with the organization's strategy and goals

C) To manage the budget and resources for the Agile Release Train

D) To define the acceptance criteria for the solution

Answer: B) To ensure alignment with the organization's strategy and goals

Explanation: The Business Owner plays a key role in the Lean-Agile Enterprise by ensuring alignment with the organization's strategy and goals, and that the solution meets customer needs and expectations.

Question 40

Which of the following is a key aspect of SAFe's Relentless Improvement?

A) Focusing on efficiency and reducing waste

B) Emphasizing predictability and control over adaptability

C) Encouraging experimentation and learning from failure

D) Prioritizing individual performance over team performance

Answer: C) Encouraging experimentation and learning from failure

Explanation: SAFe's Relentless Improvement emphasizes encouraging experimentation and learning from failure, enabling organizations to continuously improve and adapt to changing market conditions, and to innovate and deliver value to customers.

Question 41

In SAFe, what is the purpose of the Solution Context?

A) To define the technical architecture of the solution

B) To identify the key stakeholders and their needs

C) To establish the program's goals and objectives

D) To understand the solution's operating environment and constraints

Answer: D) To understand the solution's operating environment and constraints

Explanation: The Solution Context is a critical aspect of SAFe that helps teams understand the solution's operating environment and constraints, ensuring that the solution meets customer needs and fits within the organization's existing infrastructure.

Question 42

Which of the following is a key benefit of implementing SAFe's Agile Release Trains (ARTs)?

A) Improved collaboration and communication among teams

B) Enhanced predictability and reduced variability

C) Increased efficiency through automation

D) Ability to manage multiple programs and value streams

Answer: D) Ability to manage multiple programs and value streams

Explanation: SAFe's Agile Release Trains (ARTs) enable organizations to manage multiple programs and value streams, ensuring that the work is properly coordinated and aligned, and that the organization is delivering value to customers efficiently and effectively.

Question 43

In SAFe, what is the role of the Release Train Engineer (RTE) in managing dependencies?

A) To identify and prioritize dependencies

B) To manage and resolve dependencies

C) To communicate dependencies to stakeholders

D) To eliminate dependencies

Answer: B) To manage and resolve dependencies

Explanation: The Release Train Engineer (RTE) plays a key role in managing dependencies by identifying, prioritizing, and resolving them, ensuring that the Agile Release Train (ART) can deliver value to customers efficiently and effectively.

Question 44

Which of the following is a key aspect of SAFe's Lean-Agile Metrics?

A) Measuring individual performance and velocity

B) Tracking progress and flow through the Continuous Delivery Pipeline

C) Monitoring budget and resource utilization

D) Comparing teams' performance and velocity

Answer: B) Tracking progress and flow through the Continuous Delivery Pipeline

Explanation: SAFe's Lean-Agile Metrics emphasize tracking progress and flow through the Continuous Delivery Pipeline, enabling organizations to measure the effectiveness of their Lean-Agile practices and identify areas for improvement.

Question 45

In SAFe, what is the purpose of the Program Kanban's WIP Limits?

A) To prioritize the Program Backlog

B) To manage the flow of work across teams

C) To limit the amount of work in progress to ensure focus and efficiency

D) To assign work to individual Agile Teams

Answer: C) To limit the amount of work in progress to ensure focus and efficiency

Explanation: The Program Kanban's WIP (Work in Progress) Limits are used to limit the amount of work in progress, ensuring that teams focus on high-priority items and deliver value efficiently.

PRACTICE TEST - 2

Question 46

Which of the following is a key benefit of implementing SAFe's DevOps and Continuous Delivery?

A) Improved collaboration and communication among teams

B) Enhanced predictability and reduced variability

C) Increased speed and efficiency in delivering value to customers

D) Ability to manage complex programs with multiple dependencies

Answer: C) Increased speed and efficiency in delivering value to customers

Explanation: SAFe's DevOps and Continuous Delivery enable organizations to deliver value to customers faster and more efficiently, reducing the time and effort required to release new features and improvements.

Question 47

In SAFe, what is the role of the Agile Team's Scrum Master in the Program Increment (PI) Planning?

A) To facilitate the team's iteration planning

B) To ensure the team's work aligns with the program's goals

C) To prioritize the Program Backlog

D) To manage the team's dependencies with other teams

Answer: B) To ensure the team's work aligns with the program's goals

Explanation: The Agile Team's Scrum Master plays a key role in PI Planning by ensuring the team's work aligns with the program's goals and objectives, and that the team is working towards a common objective.

Question 48

Which of the following is a key aspect of SAFe's Lean-Agile Leadership?

A) Emphasizing predictability and control over adaptability

B) Focusing on individual performance over team performance

C) Encouraging experimentation and learning from failure

D) Prioritizing efficiency and reducing waste

Answer: C) Encouraging experimentation and learning from failure

Explanation: SAFe's Lean-Agile Leadership emphasizes encouraging experimentation and learning from failure, enabling organizations to continuously improve and adapt to changing market conditions, and to innovate and deliver value to customers.

Question 49

In SAFe, what is the purpose of the Solution Demo's Iteration Goals?

A) To define the solution's architecture

B) To prioritize the Program Backlog

C) To ensure alignment with the program's goals and objectives

D) To provide feedback to the Agile Teams

Answer: C) To ensure alignment with the program's goals and objectives

Explanation: The Solution Demo's Iteration Goals ensure alignment with the program's goals and objectives, providing a clear understanding of the solution's progress and ensuring that the Agile Teams are working towards a common objective

Question 50

Which of the following is a key benefit of implementing SAFe's Continuous Improvement?

A) Improved collaboration and communication among teams

B) Enhanced predictability and reduced variability

C) Increased speed and efficiency in delivering value to customers

D) Ability to identify and address systemic impediments

Answer: D) Ability to identify and address systemic impediments

Explanation: SAFe's Continuous Improvement enables organizations to identify and address systemic impediments, ensuring that the organization can continuously improve and adapt to changing market conditions, and deliver value to customers efficiently and effectively.

Question 51

In SAFe, what is the role of the Release Train Engineer (RTE) in facilitating Program Level Events?

A) To prioritize the Program Backlog

B) To ensure alignment with the program's goals and objectives

C) To facilitate events such as PI Planning and Inspect and Adapt

D) To manage the program's budget and resources

Answer: C) To facilitate events such as PI Planning and Inspect and Adapt

Explanation: The Release Train Engineer (RTE) plays a key role in facilitating Program Level Events such as PI Planning and Inspect and Adapt, ensuring that these events are successful and that the program's goals and objectives are met.

Question 52

Which of the following is a key aspect of SAFe's Lean Portfolio Management (LPM)?

A) Prioritizing projects based on business value

B) Managing programs and value streams

C) Aligning portfolio vision with enterprise strategy

D) All of the above

Answer: D) All of the above

Explanation: SAFe's Lean Portfolio Management (LPM) involves prioritizing projects based on business value, managing programs and value streams, and aligning portfolio vision with enterprise strategy, ensuring that the organization's portfolio is aligned with its overall strategy and goals.

Question 53

A new Agile Release Train (ART) is being formed, and the teams are struggling to align their work with the program's goals and objectives. Which of the following actions should the Release Train Engineer (RTE) take to facilitate alignment?

A) Conduct a series of one-on-one meetings with each team's Scrum Master to discuss their concerns

B) Facilitate a program-level event to align the teams' work with the program's goals and objectives

C) Work with the Product Management team to prioritize the Program Backlog

D) Develop a detailed project plan to ensure alignment

Answer: B) Facilitate a program-level event to align the teams' work with the program's goals and objectives

Explanation: The RTE should facilitate a program-level event, such as a PI Planning session, to align the teams' work with the program's goals and objectives. This event brings together all teams and stakeholders to ensure everyone is working towards a common objective.

Question 54

An Agile Team is experiencing significant delays in delivering value to customers due to dependencies on other teams. Which of the following actions should the Scrum Master take to address the issue?

A) Work with the team to develop a detailed project plan to manage dependencies

B) Collaborate with the other teams' Scrum Masters to resolve dependencies

C) Escalate the issue to the Release Train Engineer (RTE) for resolution

D) Focus on improving the team's velocity to compensate for delays

Answer: B) Collaborate with the other teams' Scrum Masters to resolve dependencies

Explanation: The Scrum Master should collaborate with the other teams' Scrum Masters to resolve dependencies, ensuring that the teams are working together to deliver value to customers. This collaboration can help identify and address systemic impediments.

Question 55

A large enterprise is implementing SAFe to scale Agile across multiple teams and programs. However, the organization's leadership is concerned about the potential overhead of adopting SAFe. Which of the following strategies should the SAFe Program Consultant use to address leadership's concerns?

A) Emphasize the benefits of SAFe in terms of increased efficiency and reduced costs

B) Highlight the importance of adopting SAFe to stay competitive in the market

C) Focus on the value of SAFe in improving collaboration and alignment across teams and programs

D) Provide case studies of successful SAFe implementations in similar industries

Answer: C) Focus on the value of SAFe in improving collaboration and alignment across teams and programs

Explanation: The SAFe Program Consultant should focus on the value of SAFe in improving collaboration and alignment across teams and programs, highlighting how SAFe can help address the organization's specific pain points and improve overall delivery of value to customers.

Question 56

An Agile Release Train (ART) is struggling to meet its commitments due to inconsistent velocity across teams. Which of the following actions should the Release Train Engineer (RTE) take to address the issue?

A) Work with each team to develop a customized iteration plan

B) Implement a standardized iteration plan across all teams

C) Focus on improving the ART's overall velocity by identifying and addressing systemic impediments

D) Adjust the team's iteration lengths to better align with their velocity

Answer: C) Focus on improving the ART's overall velocity by identifying and addressing systemic impediments

Explanation: The RTE should focus on improving the ART's overall velocity by identifying and addressing systemic impediments, rather than trying to control or standardize individual team velocities. This approach helps to address the root causes of inconsistent velocity and improve the ART's overall delivery of value.

Question 57

A SAFe organization is experiencing challenges with integrating new teams into an existing Agile Release Train (ART). Which of the following strategies should the Release Train Engineer (RTE) use to facilitate a smooth integration?

A) Conduct a comprehensive training program for new teams on SAFe principles and practices

B) Pair new teams with experienced teams for mentorship and guidance

C) Develop a customized onboarding plan for new teams, including tailored training and coaching

D) Require new teams to adopt the same processes and practices as existing teams

Answer: C) Develop a customized onboarding plan for new teams, including tailored training and coaching

Explanation: The RTE should develop a customized onboarding plan for new teams, including tailored training and coaching, to ensure a smooth integration into the existing ART. This approach recognizes that each team has unique needs and requirements.

Question 58

An Agile Team within a SAFe organization is struggling to refine its backlog due to unclear requirements and priorities. Which of the following actions should the Product Owner take to address the issue?

A) Work with stakeholders to develop a comprehensive product roadmap

B) Collaborate with the team to refine the backlog through workshops and brainstorming sessions

C) Develop a detailed product requirements document (PRD) to clarify requirements

D) Prioritize the backlog based on business value and customer needs

Answer: B) Collaborate with the team to refine the backlog through workshops and brainstorming sessions

Explanation: The Product Owner should collaborate with the team to refine the backlog through workshops and brainstorming sessions, ensuring that the team has a clear understanding of requirements and priorities. This approach encourages active participation and ownership.

Question 59

A SAFe organization is implementing a new Agile Release Train (ART) to support a critical business initiative. However, the ART is struggling to align with the organization's overall strategy and goals. Which of the following actions should the Release Train Engineer (RTE) take to address the issue?

A) Conduct a series of meetings with stakeholders to clarify the organization's strategy and goals

B) Develop a detailed program charter to outline the ART's objectives and deliverables

C) Facilitate a strategic alignment workshop with the ART and stakeholders to ensure alignment

D) Establish a set of metrics to measure the ART's progress and alignment

Answer: C) Facilitate a strategic alignment workshop with the ART and stakeholders to ensure alignment

Explanation: The RTE should facilitate a strategic alignment workshop with the ART and stakeholders to ensure alignment, bringing together key stakeholders to clarify the organization's strategy and goals and ensure the ART is working towards a common objective.

Question 60

An Agile Team within a SAFe organization is experiencing significant delays in delivering value to customers due to complex dependencies with other teams. Which of the following actions should the Scrum Master take to address the issue?

A) Work with the team to develop a detailed dependency management plan

B) Collaborate with other teams' Scrum Masters to resolve dependencies through joint planning and coordination

C) Establish a dependency management board to track and manage dependencies

D) Focus on improving the team's velocity to compensate for delays

Answer: B) Collaborate with other teams' Scrum Masters to resolve dependencies through joint planning and coordination

Explanation: The Scrum Master should collaborate with other teams' Scrum Masters to resolve dependencies through joint planning and coordination, ensuring that teams are working together to deliver value to customers efficiently and effectively.

Question 61

A SAFe organization is experiencing challenges with scaling Agile practices across multiple teams and programs. Which of the following actions should the SAFe Program Consultant take to address the issue?

A) Conduct a comprehensive assessment of the organization's Agile maturity

B) Develop a customized SAFe implementation plan tailored to the organization's needs

C) Provide training and coaching to teams and leaders on SAFe principles and practices

D) Establish a SAFe Center of Excellence to promote Agile best practices

Answer: B) Develop a customized SAFe implementation plan tailored to the organization's needs

Explanation: The SAFe Program Consultant should develop a customized SAFe implementation plan tailored to the organization's needs, recognizing that each organization has unique challenges and requirements.

Question 62

An Agile Release Train (ART) is struggling to deliver value to customers due to inconsistent quality practices across teams. Which of the following actions should the Release Train Engineer (RTE) take to address the issue?

A) Establish a quality management office to oversee quality practices

B) Develop a comprehensive quality management plan for the ART

C) Collaborate with teams to establish common quality practices and standards

D) Conduct regular quality audits to ensure compliance

Answer: C) Collaborate with teams to establish common quality practices and standards

Explanation: The RTE should collaborate with teams to establish common quality practices and standards, ensuring that teams are working together to deliver high-quality solutions to customers.

Question 63

During Iteration Planning, an Agile Team is struggling to align on a shared understanding of the iteration goals and objectives. Which of the following actions should the Scrum Master take to facilitate alignment?

A) Conduct a team workshop to clarify iteration goals and objectives

B) Work with the Product Owner to refine the backlog items

C) Establish a set of iteration goals and objectives without team input

D) Proceed with iteration planning without alignment

Answer: A) Conduct a team workshop to clarify iteration goals and objectives

Explanation: The Scrum Master should conduct a team workshop to clarify iteration goals and objectives, ensuring that the team has a shared understanding of what needs to be accomplished during the iteration.

Question 64

During the Iteration Review, an Agile Team is having difficulty demonstrating progress to stakeholders due to incomplete work. Which of the following actions should the Scrum Master take to address the issue?

A) Work with the team to develop a plan to complete the incomplete work

B) Conduct a retrospective to identify root causes of incomplete work

C) Focus on demonstrating completed work and ignore incomplete work

D) Cancel the Iteration Review

Answer: A) Work with the team to develop a plan to complete the incomplete work

Explanation: The Scrum Master should work with the team to develop a plan to complete the incomplete work, ensuring that the team can demonstrate progress to stakeholders and deliver value to customers.

Question 65

During Backlog Refinement, an Agile Team is struggling to estimate the size of backlog items due to lack of understanding of the requirements. Which of the following actions should the Scrum Master take to facilitate estimation?

A) Work with the Product Owner to provide more detailed requirements

B) Conduct a workshop with the team to clarify requirements and estimate size

C) Use historical data to estimate the size of backlog items

D) Assign a single team member to estimate the size of backlog items

Answer: B) Conduct a workshop with the team to clarify requirements and estimate size

Explanation: The Scrum Master should conduct a workshop with the team to clarify requirements and estimate size, ensuring that the team has a shared understanding of the requirements and can accurately estimate the size of backlog items.

Question 66

During the Iteration Retrospective, an Agile Team identifies a significant impediment that is impacting their ability to deliver value to customers. Which of the following actions should the Scrum Master take to address the impediment?

A) Work with the team to develop a plan to address the impediment

B) Escalate the impediment to the Release Train Engineer (RTE) for resolution

C) Ignore the impediment and focus on iteration planning

D) Conduct a root cause analysis to identify the source of the impediment

Answer: A) Work with the team to develop a plan to address the impediment

Explanation: The Scrum Master should work with the team to develop a plan to address the impediment, empowering the team to take ownership of resolving the issue and improving their delivery of value to customers.

Question 67

During Team Sync, an Agile Team is having difficulty aligning on priorities due to conflicting stakeholder demands. Which of the following actions should the Scrum Master take to facilitate alignment?

A) Work with the Product Owner to develop a prioritized backlog

B) Conduct a stakeholder management workshop to clarify priorities

C) Use a prioritization framework to objectively determine priorities

D) Allow each stakeholder to prioritize their own backlog items

Answer: B) Conduct a stakeholder management workshop to clarify priorities

Explanation: The Scrum Master should conduct a stakeholder management workshop to clarify priorities, ensuring that the team understands the needs and expectations of all stakeholders and can align on a shared set of priorities.

Question 68

During Iteration Planning, an Agile Team is struggling to allocate capacity due to uncertain team availability. Which of the following actions should the Scrum Master take to facilitate capacity allocation?

A) Work with the team to develop a capacity allocation plan based on historical data

B) Conduct a team workshop to clarify availability and allocate capacity

C) Use a capacity allocation tool to objectively determine allocation

D) Allow each team member to allocate their own capacity

Answer: B) Conduct a team workshop to clarify availability and allocate capacity

Explanation: The Scrum Master should conduct a team workshop to clarify availability and allocate capacity, ensuring that the team has a shared understanding of availability and can allocate capacity effectively to meet iteration goals.

Question 69

During Iteration Planning, an Agile Team is having difficulty meeting the iteration goals due to overly ambitious planning. Which of the following actions should the Scrum Master take to facilitate realistic planning?

A) Work with the team to decompose large backlog items into smaller ones

B) Conduct a team workshop to clarify iteration goals and constraints

C) Use historical data to determine a realistic velocity

D) Allow the team to commit to the ambitious plan

Answer: C) Use historical data to determine a realistic velocity

Explanation: The Scrum Master should use historical data to determine a realistic velocity, ensuring that the team's iteration plan is aligned with their actual capacity and ability to deliver.

Question 70

During the Iteration Retrospective, an Agile Team identifies a significant improvement opportunity related to their development practices. Which of the following actions should the Scrum Master take to facilitate improvement?

A) Work with the team to develop an action plan to address the improvement opportunity

B) Conduct a workshop with the team to explore alternative development practices

C) Bring in an external expert to provide guidance on development practices

D) Document the improvement opportunity and wait for next retrospective

Answer: A) Work with the team to develop an action plan to address the improvement opportunity

Explanation: The Scrum Master should work with the team to develop an action plan to address the improvement opportunity, empowering the team to take ownership of their own improvement and implement changes to their development practices.

Question 71

During Backlog Refinement, an Agile Team is struggling to clarify acceptance criteria for a complex backlog item. Which of the following actions should the Scrum Master take to facilitate clarification?

A) Work with the Product Owner to develop a clear product description

B) Conduct a workshop with the team and stakeholders to clarify acceptance criteria

C) Use a requirements clarification framework to guide the discussion

D) Allow the team to assume acceptance criteria based on their understanding

Answer: B) Conduct a workshop with the team and stakeholders to clarify acceptance criteria

Explanation: The Scrum Master should conduct a workshop with the team and stakeholders to clarify acceptance criteria, ensuring that everyone has a shared understanding of what constitutes "done" for the complex backlog item.

Question 72

During the Iteration Review, an Agile Team is having difficulty demonstrating progress to stakeholders due to lack of visibility into their work. Which of the following actions should the Scrum Master take to facilitate visibility?

A) Work with the team to develop a dashboard to track progress

B) Conduct a workshop with the team to identify and address visibility gaps

C) Use a project management tool to track and report progress

D) Provide a detailed report of progress to stakeholders

Answer: B) Conduct a workshop with the team to identify and address visibility gaps

Explanation: The Scrum Master should conduct a workshop with the team to identify and address visibility gaps, empowering the team to take ownership of their own visibility and ensure that stakeholders have a clear understanding of their progress.

Question 73

During PI Planning, an Agile Release Train (ART) is struggling to align on a shared understanding of the Program Increment (PI) objectives. Which of the following actions should the Release Train Engineer (RTE) take to facilitate alignment?

A) Conduct a workshop with the ART to clarify PI objectives

B) Work with the Product Management team to refine the PI objectives

C) Use a PI objective template to standardize the objectives

D) Allow each team to define their own PI objectives

Answer: A) Conduct a workshop with the ART to clarify PI objectives

Explanation: The RTE should conduct a workshop with the ART to clarify PI objectives, ensuring that all teams and stakeholders have a shared understanding of the PI objectives and can align their work accordingly.

Question 74

During the Inspect and Adapt event, an Agile Release Train (ART) identifies a significant impediment related to their IP Iteration cadence. Which of the following actions should the Release Train Engineer (RTE) take to facilitate adaptation?

A) Work with the ART to develop an action plan to address the impediment

B) Conduct a workshop with the ART to explore alternative IP Iteration cadences

C) Use data and metrics to analyze the impact of the impediment

D) Delay the IP Iteration to allow for more planning time

Answer: A) Work with the ART to develop an action plan to address the impediment

Explanation: The RTE should work with the ART to develop an action plan to address the impediment, empowering the ART to take ownership of their own adaptation and implement changes to their IP Iteration cadence.

Question 75

During PI Planning, an Agile Release Train (ART) is struggling to allocate capacity across teams due to conflicting priorities. Which of the following actions should the Release Train Engineer (RTE) take to facilitate capacity allocation?

A) Conduct a capacity allocation workshop with the ART to clarify priorities

B) Work with the Product Management team to refine the program backlog

C) Use a capacity allocation tool to objectively determine allocation

D) Allow each team to allocate their own capacity

Answer: A) Conduct a capacity allocation workshop with the ART to clarify priorities

Explanation: The RTE should conduct a capacity allocation workshop with the ART to clarify priorities, ensuring that the ART has a shared understanding of priorities and can allocate capacity effectively to meet PI objectives.

Question 76

During the Inspect and Adapt event, an Agile Release Train (ART) identifies a significant opportunity to improve their IP Iteration planning process. Which of the following actions should the Release Train Engineer (RTE) take to facilitate improvement?

A) Work with the ART to develop an action plan to improve IP Iteration planning

B) Conduct a workshop with the ART to explore alternative planning approaches

C) Use data and metrics to analyze the effectiveness of the current planning process

D) Delay the next IP Iteration to allow for more planning time

Answer: A) Work with the ART to develop an action plan to improve IP Iteration planning

Explanation: The RTE should work with the ART to develop an action plan to improve IP Iteration planning, empowering the ART to take ownership of their own improvement and implement changes to their planning process.

Question 77

During PI Planning, an Agile Release Train (ART) is struggling to establish a shared understanding of the program vision and roadmap. Which of the following actions should the Release Train Engineer (RTE) take to facilitate alignment?

A) Conduct a program vision and roadmap workshop with the ART

B) Work with the Product Management team to refine the program backlog

C) Use a program vision and roadmap template to standardize the approach

D) Allow each team to define their own program vision and roadmap

Answer: A) Conduct a program vision and roadmap workshop with the ART

Explanation: The RTE should conduct a program vision and roadmap workshop with the ART, ensuring that all teams and stakeholders have a shared understanding of the program vision and roadmap and can align their work accordingly.

Question 78

During the Inspect and Adapt event, an Agile Release Train (ART) identifies a significant gap in their IP Iteration execution related to team collaboration. Which of the following actions should the Release Train Engineer (RTE) take to facilitate improvement?

A) Work with the ART to develop an action plan to improve team collaboration

B) Conduct a workshop with the ART to explore alternative collaboration approaches

C) Use data and metrics to analyze the effectiveness of current collaboration practices

D) Establish a new team to focus on collaboration improvement

Answer: A) Work with the ART to develop an action plan to improve team collaboration

Explanation: The RTE should work with the ART to develop an action plan to improve team collaboration, empowering the ART to take ownership of their own improvement and implement changes to their collaboration practices.

Question 79

During PI Planning, an Agile Release Train (ART) is struggling to identify and prioritize program-level risks. Which of the following actions should the Release Train Engineer (RTE) take to facilitate risk identification and prioritization?

A) Conduct a risk identification and prioritization workshop with the ART

B) Work with the Product Management team to refine the program backlog

C) Use a risk management framework to standardize the approach

D) Allow each team to identify and prioritize their own risks

Answer: A) Conduct a risk identification and prioritization workshop with the ART

Explanation: The RTE should conduct a risk identification and prioritization workshop with the ART, ensuring that all teams and stakeholders have a shared understanding of program-level risks and can prioritize mitigation efforts accordingly.

Question 80

During the Inspect and Adapt event, an Agile Release Train (ART) identifies a significant opportunity to improve their IP Iteration learning and innovation. Which of the following actions should the Release Train Engineer (RTE) take to facilitate improvement?

A) Work with the ART to develop an action plan to improve learning and innovation

B) Conduct a workshop with the ART to explore alternative learning and innovation approaches

C) Use data and metrics to analyze the effectiveness of current learning and innovation practices

D) Establish a new team to focus on learning and innovation improvement

Answer: A) Work with the ART to develop an action plan to improve learning and innovation

Explanation: The RTE should work with the ART to develop an action plan to improve learning and innovation, empowering the ART to take ownership of their own improvement and implement changes to their learning and innovation practices.

Question 81

A SAFe organization is implementing the Scrum Master/Team Coach role to support Agile Teams. Which of the following is the primary responsibility of the Scrum Master/Team Coach?

A) To manage and prioritize the team's backlog

B) To facilitate team events and ensure Scrum framework adherence

C) To coach and mentor Agile Teams on SAFe principles and practices

D) To manage and report team velocity and performance metrics

Answer: C) To coach and mentor Agile Teams on SAFe principles and practices

Explanation: The Scrum Master/Team Coach is responsible for coaching and mentoring Agile Teams on SAFe principles and practices, empowering them to become self-organizing and high-performing teams.

Question 82

A Scrum Master/Team Coach is working with an Agile Team to improve their delivery of value to customers. Which of the following coaching approaches should the Scrum Master/Team Coach use?

A) Directive coaching, providing explicit instructions and guidance

B) Facilitative coaching, empowering the team to self-organize and make decisions

C) Transformational coaching, focusing on organizational change and transformation

D) Transactional coaching, focusing on individual skills and knowledge development

Answer: B) Facilitative coaching, empowering the team to self-organize and make decisions

Explanation: The Scrum Master/Team Coach should use facilitative coaching, empowering the team to self-organize and make decisions, and fostering a culture of collaboration, experimentation, and continuous improvement.

Question 83

A Scrum Master/Team Coach is working with an Agile Team to improve their collaboration and communication. Which of the following actions should the Scrum Master/Team Coach take to facilitate team collaboration?

A) Conduct a team workshop to establish clear roles and responsibilities

B) Implement a communication plan to standardize team communication

C) Facilitate team events to foster collaboration and alignment

D) Provide individual coaching to team members to improve their communication skills

Answer: C) Facilitate team events to foster collaboration and alignment

Explanation: The Scrum Master/Team Coach should facilitate team events, such as team lunches, retrospectives, and planning sessions, to foster collaboration and alignment among team members.

Question 84

A Scrum Master/Team Coach is working with an Agile Team to improve their delivery of value to customers. Which of the following metrics should the Scrum Master/Team Coach use to measure team performance?

A) Team velocity and burn-down rate

B) Customer satisfaction and net promoter score

C) Team member happiness and engagement

D) Defect density and test coverage

Answer: B) Customer satisfaction and net promoter score

Explanation: The Scrum Master/Team Coach should use customer satisfaction and net promoter score to measure team performance, as these metrics directly reflect the team's ability to deliver value to customers.

Question 85

An Agile Team is implementing Continuous Integration (CI) and Continuous Delivery (CD) practices. Which of the following benefits can they expect from implementing CI/CD?

A) Faster time-to-market and reduced deployment risk

B) Improved code quality and reduced testing effort

C) Increased team velocity and reduced meeting time

D) Enhanced collaboration and improved team morale

Answer: A) Faster time-to-market and reduced deployment risk

Explanation: Implementing CI/CD practices enables Agile Teams to deliver software faster and more reliably, reducing the risk of deployment failures and improving overall quality.

Question 86

An Agile Team is using Test-Driven Development (TDD) to improve their development process. Which of the following statements best describes the primary benefit of TDD?

A) Reduced testing effort and improved code coverage

B) Improved code quality and reduced defect density

C) Faster development velocity and improved team productivity

D) Enhanced collaboration and improved team communication

Answer: B) Improved code quality and reduced defect density

Explanation: The primary benefit of TDD is improved code quality and reduced defect density, as writing tests before writing code ensures that the code is testable, reliable, and meets requirements.

Question 87

An Agile Team is implementing pair programming to improve their development process. Which of the following benefits can they expect from pair programming?

A) Improved code quality and reduced defect density

B) Increased development velocity and reduced meeting time

C) Enhanced collaboration and improved team communication

D) Reduced testing effort and improved code coverage

Answer: A) Improved code quality and reduced defect density

Explanation: Pair programming involves two developers working together on the same code, which improves code quality, reduces defect density, and enhances knowledge sharing.

Question 88

An Agile Team is using refactoring to improve their codebase. Which of the following statements best describes the primary goal of refactoring?

A) To add new features and functionality to the codebase

B) To improve code performance and efficiency

C) To simplify and clarify the codebase without changing its behavior

D) To reduce testing effort and improve code coverage

Answer: C) To simplify and clarify the codebase without changing its behavior

Explanation: Refactoring aims to simplify and clarify the codebase, making it easier to maintain, understand, and extend, without changing its external behavior.

Question 89

An Agile Team is using Agile Estimation techniques to estimate the complexity of their backlog items. Which of the following estimation techniques is most suitable for estimating large and complex backlog items?

A) Story Points

B) T-Shirt Sizing

C) Hours/Days

D) Relative Estimation

Answer: A) Story Points

Explanation: Story Points are a relative estimation technique that considers the complexity, risk, and effort required to complete a backlog item, making it suitable for estimating large and complex items.

Question 90

An Agile Team is implementing Continuous Testing practices to improve their development process. Which of the following testing practices is most effective in catching defects early in the development cycle?

A) Unit Testing

B) Integration Testing

C) System Testing

D) Acceptance Testing

Answer: A) Unit Testing

Explanation: Unit Testing involves testing individual components or units of code, which helps catch defects early in the development cycle, reducing the overall defect density and improving code quality.

PRACTICE TEST - 3

Question 91

An Agile Team is using Agile Metrics to measure their development process. Which of the following metrics is most effective in measuring team velocity and predictability?

A) Burn-down Rate

B) Cycle Time

C) Lead Time

D) Cumulative Flow Diagram (CFD)

Answer: B) Cycle Time

Explanation: Cycle Time measures the time it takes for a team to complete a backlog item from start to finish, providing insights into team velocity and predictability.

Question 92

An Agile Team is implementing Agile Design practices to improve their development process. Which of the following design practices is most effective in ensuring that the system meets the required functionality and quality attributes?

A) Test-Driven Design (TDD)

B) Domain-Driven Design (DDD)

C) Model-Driven Design (MDD)

D) Architecture-Driven Design (ADD)

Answer: B) Domain-Driven Design (DDD)

Explanation: Domain-Driven Design (DDD) focuses on understanding the core business domain and modeling the system to meet the required functionality and quality attributes, ensuring that the system meets the needs of its users.

Question 93

An Agile Team is using Agile Principles to guide their development process. Which of the following principles is most closely related to the concept of Continuous Improvement?

A) Individuals and Interactions

B) Working Software

C) Customer Collaboration

D) Responding to Change

Answer: D) Responding to Change

Explanation: The principle of Responding to Change emphasizes the importance of continuous improvement, encouraging teams to regularly reflect on their processes and adapt to changing requirements.

Question 94

An Agile Team is implementing Agile Practices to improve their development process. Which of the following practices is most closely related to the concept of Reducing Technical Debt?

A) Refactoring

B) Pair Programming

C) Test-Driven Development (TDD)

D) Continuous Integration (CI)

Answer: A) Refactoring

Explanation: Refactoring involves regularly reviewing and improving the codebase to reduce technical debt, making it easier to maintain, understand, and extend.

Question 95

An Agile Team is using Agile Manifesto values to guide their development process. Which of the following values is most closely related to the concept of prioritizing customer needs?

A) Individuals and Interactions

B) Working Software

C) Customer Collaboration

D) Responding to Change

Answer: C) Customer Collaboration

Explanation: The value of Customer Collaboration emphasizes the importance of working closely with customers to understand their needs and priorities, ensuring that the team delivers value to them.

Question 96

An Agile Team is implementing Agile Practices to improve their development process. Which of the following practices is most closely related to the concept of ensuring code quality?

A) Continuous Testing

B) Continuous Integration

C) Continuous Deployment

D) Continuous Monitoring

Answer: B) Continuous Integration

Explanation: Continuous Integration involves regularly integrating code changes into a shared repository, ensuring that the codebase is stable, and automating tests to catch defects early, thereby ensuring code quality.

Question 97

An Agile Team is using Agile Principles to guide their development process. Which of the following principles is most closely related to the concept of empowering teams to make decisions?

A) Build projects around motivated individuals

B) Give them the environment and support they need

C) Trust them to get the job done

D) Provide frequent feedback and coaching

Answer: C) Trust them to get the job done

Explanation: The principle of trusting teams to get the job done empowers them to take ownership and make decisions, encouraging autonomy and self-organization.

Question 98

An Agile Team is implementing Agile Practices to improve their development process. Which of the following practices is most closely related to the concept of visualizing workflow and identifying bottlenecks?

A) Kanban Board

B) Scrum Board

C) Burn-down Chart

D) Velocity Chart

Answer: A) Kanban Board

Explanation: A Kanban Board visualizes the workflow, showing the progress of work items through stages, and helps identify bottlenecks, enabling teams to optimize their process and improve flow.

QUESTION 99

An Agile Team is using Agile Metrics to measure their development process. Which of the following metrics is most closely related to the concept of measuring team efficiency and productivity?

A) Cycle Time

B) Lead Time

C) Throughput

D) Velocity

Answer: D) Velocity

Explanation: Velocity measures the amount of work a team can complete during a sprint, providing insights into team efficiency and productivity.

Question 100

An Agile Team is implementing Agile Practices to improve their development process. Which of the following practices is most closely related to the concept of ensuring that the team has a shared understanding of the work to be done?

A) Backlog Refinement

B) Sprint Planning

C) Daily Scrum

D) Retrospective

Answer: A) Backlog Refinement

Explanation: Backlog Refinement involves ensuring that the backlog items are clear, concise, and well-understood by the team, fostering a shared understanding of the work to be done.

Question 101

An Agile Team is using Agile Principles to guide their development process. Which of the following principles is most closely related to the concept of embracing change and being adaptable?

A) Embrace Change

B) Respond to Change

C) Create a Learning Environment

D) Focus on Delivering Value

Answer: B) Respond to Change

Explanation: The principle of Responding to Change emphasizes the importance of being adaptable and responsive to changing requirements and circumstances.

Question 102

An Agile Team is implementing Agile Practices to improve their development process. Which of the following practices is most closely related to the concept of ensuring that the team is continuously improving and learning?

A) Retrospective

B) Sprint Review

C) Sprint Planning

D) Daily Scrum

Answer: A) Retrospective

Explanation: A Retrospective is a practice that involves regularly reflecting on the team's process and identifying opportunities for improvement, fostering a culture of continuous learning and improvement.

Question 103

In a Scrum Team, who is responsible for ensuring that the Scrum Framework is followed and that the team is working efficiently?

A) Product Owner

B) Scrum Master

C) Development Team

D) Stakeholder

Answer: B) Scrum Master

Explanation: The Scrum Master is responsible for ensuring that the Scrum Framework is followed, facilitating Scrum events, and removing impediments to help the team work efficiently.

Question 104

What is the primary purpose of the Sprint Review in Scrum?

A) To plan the work for the next Sprint

B) To review and finalize the work done during the Sprint

C) To demonstrate the increment to stakeholders and gather feedback

D) To retrospectively analyze the team's process and identify improvements

Answer: C) To demonstrate the increment to stakeholders and gather feedback

Explanation: The Sprint Review is a Scrum event where the team demonstrates the working increment to stakeholders, gathers feedback, and ensures that the work meets the requirements and expectations.

Question 105

In Scrum, what is the term for the total amount of work that can be completed by the Development Team during a Sprint?

A) Velocity

B) Capacity

C) Sprint Goal

D) Product Backlog

Answer: A) Velocity

Explanation: Velocity measures the total amount of work that can be completed by the Development Team during a Sprint, usually measured in Story Points or hours.

Question 106

Which Scrum event is time-boxed to 15 minutes and is held daily to ensure that the Development Team is on track to meet the Sprint Goal?

A) Sprint Planning

B) Daily Scrum

C) Sprint Review

D) Sprint Retrospective

Answer: B) Daily Scrum

Explanation: The Daily Scrum is a time-boxed event (15 minutes) held daily, where the Development Team reviews progress, discusses plans, and identifies impediments to ensure they are on track to meet the Sprint Goal.

Question 107

In Scrum, what is the purpose of the Product Backlog Refinement?

A) To create a detailed project plan

B) To estimate the effort required for each Product Backlog item

C) To ensure the Product Backlog is up-to-date, refined, and ready for Sprint Planning

D) To prioritize the Product Backlog items based on business value

Answer: C) To ensure the Product Backlog is up-to-date, refined, and ready for Sprint Planning

Explanation: Product Backlog Refinement is the process of ensuring the Product Backlog is up-to-date, refined, and ready for Sprint Planning, involving activities like estimating, clarifying, and prioritizing Product Backlog items.

Question 108

Which Scrum role is responsible for ensuring that the Product Backlog is visible, transparent, and clear to all stakeholders?

A) Product Owner

B) Scrum Master

C) Development Team

D) Stakeholder

Answer: A) Product Owner

Explanation: The Product Owner is responsible for ensuring that the Product Backlog is visible, transparent, and clear to all stakeholders, including the Development Team, Scrum Master, and other stakeholders.

Question 109

In Scrum, what is the term for the process of moving a Product Backlog item from the Sprint Backlog to "Done"?

A) Sprinting

B) Iterating

C) Refining

D) Releasing

Answer: B) Iterating

Explanation: In Scrum, iterating refers to the process of moving a Product Backlog item from the Sprint Backlog to "Done", involving the Development Team's work to complete the item during the Sprint.

Question 110

Which Scrum artifact provides a shared understanding of the work to be done during a Sprint?

A) Product Backlog

B) Sprint Backlog

C) Increment

D) Burn-down Chart

Answer: B) Sprint Backlog

Explanation: The Sprint Backlog provides a shared understanding of the work to be done during a Sprint, including the Product Backlog items selected for the Sprint and the tasks required to complete them.

Question 111

In Scrum, what is the purpose of the Definition of Done (DoD)?

A) To define the acceptance criteria for each Product Backlog item

B) To ensure that the Development Team has the necessary skills and expertise

C) To provide a shared understanding of what it means for work to be complete

D) To estimate the effort required for each Sprint

Answer: C) To provide a shared understanding of what it means for work to be complete

Explanation: The Definition of Done (DoD) provides a shared understanding of what it means for work to be complete, ensuring that the Development Team and stakeholders have a common understanding of quality and completeness.

Question 112

Which Scrum event is focused on identifying and addressing impediments that obstruct the Development Team's progress?

A) Sprint Planning

B) Daily Scrum

C) Sprint Review

D) Sprint Retrospective

Answer: D) Sprint Retrospective

Explanation: The Sprint Retrospective is focused on identifying and addressing impediments that obstruct the Development Team's progress, with the goal of improving processes and practices for future Sprints.

Question 113

In Scrum, what is the term for the process of breaking down large Product Backlog items into smaller, more manageable pieces?

A) Refactoring

B) Re-estimation

C) Decomposition

D) Prioritization

Answer: C) Decomposition

Explanation: Decomposition is the process of breaking down large Product Backlog items into smaller, more manageable pieces, making it easier for the Development Team to understand and estimate the work required.

Question 114

Which Scrum principle emphasizes the importance of transparency, inspection, and adaptation in the development process?

A) Empiricism

B) Self-organization

C) Continuous improvement

D) Iterative development

Answer: A) Empiricism

Explanation: Empiricism is a Scrum principle that emphasizes the importance of transparency, inspection, and adaptation in the development process, recognizing that knowledge comes from experience and experimentation.

Question 115

In a SAFe enterprise, what is the primary role of an Agile Team?

A) To implement SAFe practices and principles across the organization

B) To deliver incremental value to customers through iterative development

C) To provide governance and oversight for Agile development teams

D) To manage and prioritize the enterprise backlog

Answer: B) To deliver incremental value to customers through iterative development

Explanation: In a SAFe enterprise, Agile Teams are responsible for delivering incremental value to customers through iterative development, focusing on producing working software and continuous improvement.

QUESTION 116

In SAFe, which team is responsible for aligning the work of multiple Agile Teams to achieve a common goal?

A) Agile Team

B) Scrum Master Team

C) Product Owner Team

D) Release Train Engineer (RTE) Team

Answer: D) Release Train Engineer (RTE) Team

Explanation: In SAFe, the Release Train Engineer (RTE) Team is responsible for aligning the work of multiple Agile Teams to achieve a common goal, facilitating communication, and ensuring the successful delivery of the program increment.

Question 117

In a SAFe enterprise, what is the purpose of the Program Increment (PI) Planning event?

A) To plan and commit to a specific set of work for the next iteration

B) To review and demo the work completed during the previous iteration

C) To align teams and stakeholders around a shared vision and goals for the next program increment

D) To identify and resolve dependencies and impediments across teams

Answer: C) To align teams and stakeholders around a shared vision and goals for the next program increment

Explanation: The Program Increment (PI) Planning event in SAFe is designed to align teams and stakeholders around a shared vision and goals for the next program increment, ensuring everyone is working towards the same objectives.

Question 118

In SAFe, which role is responsible for facilitating the PI Planning event and ensuring that the teams have a clear understanding of the program vision and objectives?

A) Release Train Engineer (RTE)

B) Product Owner

C) Scrum Master

D) Business Owner

Answer: A) Release Train Engineer (RTE)

Explanation: The Release Train Engineer (RTE) is responsible for facilitating the PI Planning event, ensuring that teams have a clear understanding of the program vision and objectives, and helping to resolve dependencies and impediments.

Question 119

In a SAFe enterprise, what is the primary purpose of the System Demo?

A) To showcase the work of individual Agile Teams

B) To demonstrate the integrated system capabilities to stakeholders

C) To review and discuss the program's progress and metrics

D) To identify and resolve system-level defects and issues

Answer: B) To demonstrate the integrated system capabilities to stakeholders

Explanation: The System Demo in SAFe is designed to demonstrate the integrated system capabilities to stakeholders, providing a comprehensive view of the system's progress and value delivery.

Question 120

In SAFe, which artifact provides a visual representation of the program's progress and value delivery?

A) Program Board

B) Team Board

C) System Demo

D) Solution Demo

Answer: A) Program Board

Explanation: The Program Board in SAFe provides a visual representation of the program's progress and value delivery, showing the flow of work across teams and the program's progress towards its objectives.

Question 121

In a SAFe enterprise, what is the role of the Business Owner in the Lean-Agile Enterprise?

A) To prioritize the Program Backlog and ensure alignment with business objectives

B) To provide technical guidance and oversight to Agile Teams

C) To facilitate communication and collaboration between Agile Teams and stakeholders

D) To manage and allocate resources across Agile Teams

Answer: A) To prioritize the Program Backlog and ensure alignment with business objectives

Explanation: The Business Owner in SAFe is responsible for prioritizing the Program Backlog and ensuring alignment with business objectives, providing strategic guidance and direction to Agile Teams.

Question 122

In SAFe, which event is used to review and assess the program's progress and value delivery at the end of each Program Increment?

A) PI Planning

B) System Demo

C) Inspect and Adapt

D) Solution Demo

Answer: C) Inspect and Adapt

Explanation: The Inspect and Adapt event in SAFe is used to review and assess the program's progress and value delivery at the end of each Program Increment, identifying areas for improvement and adapting the program's direction as needed.

Question 123

In a SAFe enterprise, what is the primary purpose of the Solution Demo?

A) To demonstrate the integrated system capabilities to stakeholders

B) To review and discuss the program's progress and metrics

C) To showcase the work of individual Agile Teams

D) To demonstrate the end-to-end solution capabilities to stakeholders

Answer: D) To demonstrate the end-to-end solution capabilities to stakeholders

Explanation: The Solution Demo in SAFe is designed to demonstrate the end-to-end solution capabilities to stakeholders, providing a comprehensive view of the solution's progress and value delivery.

Question 124

In SAFe, which role is responsible for facilitating the Continuous Delivery Pipeline (CDP) and ensuring the smooth flow of value through the pipeline?

A) Release Train Engineer (RTE)

B) Product Owner

C) Scrum Master

D) DevOps Engineer

Answer: A) Release Train Engineer (RTE)

Explanation: The Release Train Engineer (RTE) in SAFe is responsible for facilitating the Continuous Delivery Pipeline (CDP) and ensuring the smooth flow of value through the pipeline, working closely with Agile Teams, Product Owners, and other stakeholders.

Question 125

In a SAFe enterprise, what is the primary benefit of implementing the Lean Portfolio Management (LPM) function?

A) To improve the efficiency of Agile Teams

B) To enhance the effectiveness of Program Increment (PI) Planning

C) To align portfolio strategy with enterprise strategy and goals

D) To streamline the flow of work through the Continuous Delivery Pipeline

Answer: C) To align portfolio strategy with enterprise strategy and goals

Explanation: The primary benefit of implementing Lean Portfolio Management (LPM) in SAFe is to align portfolio strategy with enterprise strategy and goals, ensuring that investments are aligned with business objectives.

Question 126

In SAFe, which metric is used to measure the flow of value through the Continuous Delivery Pipeline (CDP)?

A) Lead Time

B) Cycle Time

C) Value Stream Lead Time

D) Release Rate

Answer: C) Value Stream Lead Time

Explanation: Value Stream Lead Time is the metric used in SAFe to measure the flow of value through the Continuous Delivery Pipeline (CDP), from the initial request to delivery, providing insights into the efficiency and effectiveness of the pipeline.

Question 127

In a SAFe enterprise, what is the primary role of the Enterprise Architect?

A) To define and implement the technology strategy

B) To align the technology strategy with business objectives

C) To ensure compliance with regulatory requirements

D) To manage the technical debt of Agile Teams

Answer: B) To align the technology strategy with business objectives

Explanation: The primary role of the Enterprise Architect in SAFe is to align the technology strategy with business objectives, ensuring that the technology solutions support the achievement of business goals.

Question 128

In SAFe, which activity is focused on identifying and mitigating risks that could impact the program's ability to deliver value?

A) Program Backlog Refinement

B) Program Increment Planning

C) Risk Management

D) Continuous Integration

Answer: C) Risk Management

Explanation: Risk Management in SAFe is focused on identifying and mitigating risks that could impact the program's ability to deliver value, ensuring that proactive measures are taken to minimize the impact of potential risks.

Question 129

In a SAFe enterprise, what is the primary purpose of the Lean-Agile Center of Excellence (LACE)?

A) To provide training and coaching to Agile Teams

B) To support the implementation of SAFe practices and principles

C) To drive continuous improvement and innovation across the enterprise

D) To manage the Agile transformation initiative

Answer: C) To drive continuous improvement and innovation across the enterprise

Explanation: The primary purpose of the Lean-Agile Center of Excellence (LACE) in SAFe is to drive continuous improvement and innovation across the enterprise, fostering a culture of lean-agile mindset and practices.

Question 130

In SAFe, which artifact provides a high-level view of the program's progress and value delivery, highlighting achievements and areas for improvement?

A) Program Board

B) Solution Board

C) Program Progress Report

D) Inspect and Adapt Report

Answer: C) Program Progress Report

Explanation: The Program Progress Report in SAFe provides a high-level view of the program's progress and value delivery, highlighting achievements and areas for improvement, and is used to facilitate communication and transparency across stakeholders.

Question 131

In a SAFe enterprise, what is the primary responsibility of the Agile Team's Product Owner regarding the Program Backlog?

A) To prioritize the Program Backlog items based on business value

B) To ensure the Program Backlog items are aligned with the team's iteration goals

C) To refine and elaborate the top-priority Program Backlog items

D) To assign tasks to team members for Program Backlog item implementation

Answer: C) To refine and elaborate the top-priority Program Backlog items

Explanation: The Agile Team's Product Owner is responsible for refining and elaborating the top-priority Program Backlog items, ensuring they are clear, concise, and ready for implementation.

Question 132

In SAFe, which event is used to assess the program's ability to deliver value to customers and identify areas for improvement?

A) PI Planning

B) Inspect and Adapt

C) System Demo

D) Solution Demo

Answer: B) Inspect and Adapt

Explanation: The Inspect and Adapt event in SAFe is used to assess the program's ability to deliver value to customers, identify areas for improvement, and adapt the program's direction as needed.

Question 133

In a SAFe enterprise, what is the primary goal of the Agile Team's Iteration Retrospective?

A) To identify and prioritize new Program Backlog items

B) To refine and elaborate the top-priority Program Backlog items

C) To improve the team's processes and practices for the next iteration

D) To review and demo the work completed during the iteration

Answer: C) To improve the team's processes and practices for the next iteration

Explanation: The primary goal of the Agile Team's Iteration Retrospective in SAFe is to improve the team's processes and practices for the next iteration, fostering continuous improvement and learning.

Question 134

In SAFe, which role is responsible for facilitating the coordination of multiple Agile Teams and ensuring the alignment of their work with the program's objectives?

A) Release Train Engineer (RTE)

B) Scrum Master

C) Product Owner

D) Agile Team Coach

Answer: A) Release Train Engineer (RTE)

Explanation: The Release Train Engineer (RTE) in SAFe is responsible for facilitating the coordination of multiple Agile Teams and ensuring the alignment of their work with the program's objectives, enabling effective collaboration and delivery.

Question 135

In a SAFe enterprise, what is the primary purpose of the Program Kanban?

A) To visualize the flow of work across Agile Teams

B) To prioritize the Program Backlog items based on business value

C) To manage dependencies and flow of work between teams

D) To track progress and velocity of individual Agile Teams

Answer: C) To manage dependencies and flow of work between teams

Explanation: The primary purpose of the Program Kanban in SAFe is to manage dependencies and flow of work between teams, providing a visual representation of the program's workflow and enabling effective coordination and collaboration.

PRACTICE TEST - 4

Question 136

In SAFe, which practice is used to ensure that Agile Teams have a clear understanding of the program's goals and objectives?

A) Program Backlog Refinement

B) Iteration Planning

C) Program Increment Planning

D) Agile Team Alignment

Answer: C) Program Increment Planning

Explanation: Program Increment Planning in SAFe is used to ensure that Agile Teams have a clear understanding of the program's goals and objectives, aligning teams around a shared vision and goals for the program increment.

Question 137

In a SAFe enterprise, what is the primary role of the Agile Team's Scrum Master regarding the team's processes and practices?

A) To enforce SAFe practices and procedures

B) To coach the team on lean-agile principles and practices

C) To manage the team's iteration schedule and deadlines

D) To prioritize the team's backlog and ensure alignment with program goals

Answer: B) To coach the team on lean-agile principles and practices

Explanation: The Agile Team's Scrum Master in SAFe is responsible for coaching the team on lean-agile principles and practices, facilitating continuous improvement and empowering the team to take ownership of their processes.

Question 138

In SAFe, which artifact provides a comprehensive view of the program's progress and value delivery, including metrics and progress toward program goals?

A) Program Board

B) Solution Board

C) Program Progress Report

D) Program Increment Review

Answer: C) Program Progress Report

Explanation: The Program Progress Report in SAFe provides a comprehensive view of the program's progress and value delivery, including metrics and progress toward program goals, enabling stakeholders to assess program performance and make informed decisions.

Question 139

In SAFe, which characteristic is indicative of a high-performing Agile Team?

A) Strict adherence to traditional project management practices

B) Focus on individual goals and achievements over team objectives

C) Collaborative culture, embracing experimentation and learning from failure

D) Reluctance to adopt new practices and processes

Answer: C) Collaborative culture, embracing experimentation and learning from failure

Explanation: A high-performing Agile Team in SAFe exhibits a collaborative culture, embracing experimentation and learning from failure, fostering a environment of trust, transparency, and continuous improvement.

Question 140

In SAFe, what is a key indicator of a high-performing team's ability to deliver value to customers?

A) Velocity and burn-down metrics

B) Adherence to SAFe practices and procedures

C) Customer satisfaction and feedback

D) Team member satisfaction and engagement

Answer: C) Customer satisfaction and feedback

Explanation: A key indicator of a high-performing team's ability to deliver value to customers in SAFe is customer satisfaction and feedback, demonstrating that the team is delivering working solutions that meet customer needs and expectations.

Question 141

In SAFe, which characteristic is essential for a high-performing Agile Team to effectively handle changing priorities and requirements?

A) Rigidity in planning and execution

B) Resistance to new ideas and experimentation

C) Adaptability and resilience in the face of change

D) Focus on individual tasks over team goals

Answer: C) Adaptability and resilience in the face of change

Explanation: A high-performing Agile Team in SAFe exhibits adaptability and resilience in the face of change, enabling them to effectively handle changing priorities and requirements, and respond to new opportunities and challenges.

Question 142

In SAFe, what is a key factor in fostering a high-performing Agile Team's culture of continuous improvement?

A) Fear of failure and retribution

B) Encouragement of experimentation and learning from failure

C) Emphasis on individual performance over team success

D) Strict adherence to traditional processes and practices

Answer: B) Encouragement of experimentation and learning from failure

Explanation: Encouragement of experimentation and learning from failure is a key factor in fostering a high-performing Agile Team's culture of continuous improvement in SAFe, allowing team members to take risks, learn from mistakes, and drive innovation.

Question 143

In SAFe, which characteristic enables high-performing Agile Teams to effectively collaborate and align with other teams and stakeholders?

A) Focus on individual team goals over program objectives

B) Reluctance to share knowledge and expertise with other teams

C) Strong communication and interpersonal skills

D) Emphasis on traditional hierarchical structures and roles

Answer: C) Strong communication and interpersonal skills

Explanation: High-performing Agile Teams in SAFe exhibit strong communication and interpersonal skills, enabling effective collaboration and alignment with other teams and stakeholders, and fostering a culture of transparency and trust.

Question 144

In SAFe, what is a key indicator of a high-performing Agile Team's ability to drive innovation and improvement?

A) Resistance to new ideas and experimentation

B) Focus on maintaining the status quo and minimizing risk

C) Encouragement of creativity, experimentation, and learning from failure

D) Emphasis on individual performance over team success

Answer: C) Encouragement of creativity, experimentation, and learning from failure

Explanation: A key indicator of a high-performing Agile Team's ability to drive innovation and improvement in SAFe is the encouragement of creativity, experimentation, and learning from failure, allowing teams to innovate, adapt, and continuously improve.

Question 145

In SAFe, which characteristic enables high-performing Agile Teams to effectively manage conflicts and improve relationships within the team?

A) Avoidance of constructive conflict and difficult conversations

B) Focus on individual goals over team objectives

C) Emotional intelligence, empathy, and effective conflict resolution skills

D) Reluctance to share feedback and concerns

Answer: C) Emotional intelligence, empathy, and effective conflict resolution skills

Explanation: High-performing Agile Teams in SAFe exhibit emotional intelligence, empathy, and effective conflict resolution skills, enabling them to effectively manage conflicts and improve relationships within the team, and fostering a culture of trust and collaboration.

Question 146

In SAFe, what is a key factor in fostering a high-performing Agile Team's culture of continuous learning and improvement?

A) Focus on individual performance over team success

B) Resistance to new ideas and experimentation

C) Encouragement of continuous learning, knowledge sharing, and skill development

D) Emphasis on traditional hierarchical structures and roles

Answer: C) Encouragement of continuous learning, knowledge sharing, and skill development

Explanation: Encouragement of continuous learning, knowledge sharing, and skill development is a key factor in fostering a high-performing Agile Team's culture of continuous learning and improvement in SAFe, allowing teams to adapt, innovate, and continuously improve.

Question 147

In SAFe, which team event provides an opportunity for the Agile Team to align on the upcoming iteration's goals and objectives?

A) Iteration Planning

B) Daily Scrum

C) Iteration Review

D) Iteration Retrospective

Answer: A) Iteration Planning

Explanation: Iteration Planning in SAFe provides an opportunity for the Agile Team to align on the upcoming iteration's goals and objectives, ensuring everyone is aware of the work to be done and how it contributes to the program's objectives.

Question 148

In SAFe, which team event is focused on reviewing the iteration's progress, identifying areas for improvement, and adapting the process for the next iteration?

A) Iteration Planning

B) Daily Scrum

C) Iteration Review

D) Iteration Retrospective

Answer: D) Iteration Retrospective

Explanation: The Iteration Retrospective in SAFe is focused on reviewing the iteration's progress, identifying areas for improvement, and adapting the process for the next iteration, enabling continuous improvement and learning.

Question 149

In SAFe, which team event provides an opportunity for the Agile Team to demonstrate the working increment of the solution to stakeholders and receive feedback?

A) Iteration Planning

B) Daily Scrum

C) Iteration Review

D) Program Increment Review

Answer: C) Iteration Review

Explanation: The Iteration Review in SAFe provides an opportunity for the Agile Team to demonstrate the working increment of the solution to stakeholders and receive feedback, ensuring alignment and visibility into the team's progress.

Question 150

In SAFe, which team event is focused on synchronizing the team's work and ensuring everyone is aware of the progress, plans, and any obstacles?

A) Iteration Planning

B) Daily Scrum

C) Iteration Review

D) Iteration Retrospective

Answer: B) Daily Scrum

Explanation: The Daily Scrum in SAFe is focused on synchronizing the team's work and ensuring everyone is aware of the progress, plans, and any obstacles, enabling the team to collaborate and respond to changes quickly.

Question 151

In SAFe, which team event is used to review and finalize the iteration's goals and objectives, ensuring alignment with the program's objectives?

A) Iteration Planning

B) Iteration Review

C) Iteration Retrospective

D) Backlog Refinement

Answer: A) Iteration Planning

Explanation: Iteration Planning in SAFe is used to review and finalize the iteration's goals and objectives, ensuring alignment with the program's objectives, and setting the stage for the team's work during the iteration.

Question 152

In SAFe, which team event provides an opportunity for the Agile Team to reflect on their processes and practices, identifying opportunities for improvement?

A) Iteration Planning

B) Daily Scrum

C) Iteration Review

D) Iteration Retrospective

Answer: D) Iteration Retrospective

Explanation: The Iteration Retrospective in SAFe provides an opportunity for the Agile Team to reflect on their processes and practices, identifying opportunities for improvement, and implementing changes to enhance their workflow and collaboration.

Question 153

In SAFe, what is the primary purpose of the Daily Scrum event?

A) To review and demo the work completed during the iteration

B) To plan and finalize the iteration's goals and objectives

C) To synchronize the team's work and ensure everyone is aware of progress, plans, and obstacles

D) To reflect on the team's processes and practices, identifying opportunities for improvement

Answer: C) To synchronize the team's work and ensure everyone is aware of progress, plans, and obstacles

Explanation: The primary purpose of the Daily Scrum in SAFe is to synchronize the team's work and ensure everyone is aware of progress, plans, and obstacles, enabling the team to collaborate and respond to changes quickly.

Question 154

In SAFe, which event is used to review the program's progress, identify systemic issues, and develop solutions to address them?

A) Iteration Planning

B) Iteration Review

C) Iteration Retrospective

D) Program Increment Review

Answer: D) Program Increment Review

Explanation: The Program Increment Review in SAFe is used to review the program's progress, identify systemic issues, and develop solutions to address them, ensuring alignment and visibility into the program's progress and outcomes.

Question 155

In SAFe, what is the primary focus of the Iteration Review event?

A) To plan and finalize the iteration's goals and objectives

B) To review and demo the work completed during the iteration

C) To reflect on the team's processes and practices, identifying opportunities for improvement

D) To synchronize the team's work and ensure everyone is aware of progress, plans, and obstacles

Answer: B) To review and demo the work completed during the iteration

Explanation: The primary focus of the Iteration Review in SAFe is to review and demo the work completed during the iteration, ensuring alignment and visibility into the team's progress and outcomes.

Question 156

In SAFe, which event provides an opportunity for the Agile Team to refine the Program Backlog, ensuring it is up-to-date and ready for the next iteration?

A) Iteration Planning

B) Iteration Review

C) Iteration Retrospective

D) Backlog Refinement

Answer: D) Backlog Refinement

Explanation: Backlog Refinement in SAFe provides an opportunity for the Agile Team to refine the Program Backlog, ensuring it is up-to-date and ready for the next iteration, and enabling the team to effectively plan and execute their work.

Question 157

In SAFe, what is the primary outcome of the Iteration Retrospective event?

A) A refined Program Backlog, ready for the next iteration

B) A demo of the work completed during the iteration

C) A set of action items to improve the team's processes and practices

D) A set of iteration goals and objectives for the next iteration

Answer: C) A set of action items to improve the team's processes and practices

Explanation: The primary outcome of the Iteration Retrospective in SAFe is a set of action items to improve the team's processes and practices, enabling the team to continuously improve and adapt their workflow.

Question 158

In SAFe, which event is used to plan and finalize the team's work for the next iteration, ensuring alignment with the program's objectives?

A) Iteration Review

B) Iteration Retrospective

C) Backlog Refinement

D) Iteration Planning

Answer: D) Iteration Planning

Explanation: Iteration Planning in SAFe is used to plan and finalize the team's work for the next iteration, ensuring alignment with the program's objectives, and setting the stage for the team's work during the iteration.

Question 159

In SAFe, what is the primary goal of the Continuous Delivery Pipeline?

A) To automate testing and validation of the solution

B) To enable rapid release of the solution to end-users

C) To improve collaboration between Development and Operations teams

D) To reduce the risk of defects and errors in the solution

Answer: B) To enable rapid release of the solution to end-users

Explanation: The primary goal of the Continuous Delivery Pipeline in SAFe is to enable rapid release of the solution to end-users, ensuring that the solution is delivered quickly and reliably, and that the end-users receive value from the solution as soon as possible.

Question 160

In SAFe, which practice enables the Agile Release Train (ART) to release the solution to end-users at any time?

A) Continuous Integration

B) Continuous Testing

C) Continuous Deployment

D) Release on Demand

Answer: D) Release on Demand

Explanation: Release on Demand in SAFe enables the Agile Release Train (ART) to release the solution to end-users at any time, ensuring that the solution is delivered rapidly and reliably, and that the end-users receive value from the solution as soon as possible. This practice requires that the solution be in a releasable state at all times.

Question 161

In SAFe, what is the primary benefit of implementing Continuous Integration?

A) Faster time-to-market for new features and capabilities

B) Improved collaboration between Development and Operations teams

C) Reduced risk of defects and errors in the solution

D) Increased efficiency in testing and validation of the solution

Answer: C) Reduced risk of defects and errors in the solution

Explanation: The primary benefit of implementing Continuous Integration in SAFe is reduced risk of defects and errors in the solution, as it enables early detection and resolution of issues, improving the overall quality of the solution.

Question 162

In SAFe, which practice enables the Agile Release Train (ART) to ensure that the solution is releasable at any time?

A) Continuous Testing

B) Continuous Deployment

C) Continuous Monitoring

D) Continuous Verification

Answer: A) Continuous Testing

Explanation: Continuous Testing in SAFe enables the Agile Release Train (ART) to ensure that the solution is releasable at any time, by automating testing and validation of the solution, and providing immediate feedback on the quality of the solution. This practice ensures that the solution meets the required standards and is ready for release at any time.

Question 163

In SAFe, what is the primary goal of Continuous Deployment?

A) To automate testing and validation of the solution

B) To enable rapid release of the solution to end-users

C) To improve collaboration between Development and Operations teams

D) To reduce the risk of defects and errors in the solution

Answer: B) To enable rapid release of the solution to end-users

Explanation: The primary goal of Continuous Deployment in SAFe is to enable rapid release of the solution to end-users, by automating the deployment process, and ensuring that the solution is delivered quickly and reliably.

Question 164

In SAFe, which practice enables the Agile Release Train (ART) to monitor and improve the quality of the solution in production?

A) Continuous Integration

B) Continuous Testing

C) Continuous Deployment

D) Continuous Monitoring

Answer: D) Continuous Monitoring

Explanation: Continuous Monitoring in SAFe enables the Agile Release Train (ART) to monitor and improve the quality of the solution in production, by tracking key performance indicators, identifying areas for improvement, and implementing changes to enhance the solution's performance and reliability.

Question 165

In SAFe, what is the primary benefit of implementing Continuous Verification?

A) Faster time-to-market for new features and capabilities

B) Improved collaboration between Development and Operations teams

C) Reduced risk of defects and errors in the solution

D) Increased confidence in the quality of the solution

Answer: D) Increased confidence in the quality of the solution

Explanation: The primary benefit of implementing Continuous Verification in SAFe is increased confidence in the quality of the solution, as it enables automated validation of the solution against predefined criteria, ensuring that the solution meets the required standards.

Question 166

In SAFe, which practice enables the Agile Release Train (ART) to ensure that the solution is aligned with the business objectives?

A) Continuous Integration

B) Continuous Testing

C) Continuous Deployment

D) Continuous Delivery

Answer: D) Continuous Delivery

Explanation: Continuous Delivery in SAFe enables the Agile Release Train (ART) to ensure that the solution is aligned with the business objectives, by delivering the solution rapidly and reliably, and ensuring that it meets the required standards and business needs. This practice ensures that the solution is aligned with the business objectives and provides value to the end-users.

Question 167

In SAFe, what is the primary goal of the Continuous Delivery Pipeline?

A) To automate testing and validation of the solution

B) To enable rapid release of the solution to end-users

C) To improve collaboration between Development and Operations teams

D) To provide visibility into the flow of value through the system

Answer: D) To provide visibility into the flow of value through the system

Explanation: The primary goal of the Continuous Delivery Pipeline in SAFe is to provide visibility into the flow of value through the system, enabling the Agile Release Train (ART) to track the progress of the solution from development to deployment, and identify areas for improvement.

Question 168

In SAFe, which practice enables the Agile Release Train (ART) to respond quickly to changes in business requirements or market conditions?

A) Continuous Integration

B) Continuous Testing

C) Continuous Deployment

D) Release on Demand

Answer: D) Release on Demand

Explanation: Release on Demand in SAFe enables the Agile Release Train (ART) to respond quickly to changes in business requirements or market conditions, by releasing the solution to end-users at any time, and ensuring that the solution is aligned with the changing business needs.

Question 169

What is a key characteristic of a effective Scrum Master in SAFe?

A) Technical expertise in the solution being developed

B) Ability to manage and direct the Development Team

C) Coaching and facilitation skills to support the team's growth

D) Authority to make decisions on behalf of the Product Owner

Answer: C) Coaching and facilitation skills to support the team's growth

Explanation: A key characteristic of an effective Scrum Master in SAFe is coaching and facilitation skills to support the team's growth, enabling the team to become self-organizing and high-performing.

Question 170

What is a key responsibility of a Scrum Master in SAFe?

A) Prioritizing and refining the Program Backlog

B) Coordinating and managing dependencies between teams

C) Facilitating team events and coaching the team to improve

D) Tracking and reporting progress to stakeholders

Answer: C) Facilitating team events and coaching the team to improve

Explanation: A key responsibility of a Scrum Master in SAFe is facilitating team events and coaching the team to improve, ensuring that the team is working effectively and efficiently, and removing impediments to progress.

Question 171

What is the primary goal of Backlog Refinement in SAFe?

A) To prioritize the Program Backlog based on business value

B) To refine and elaborate the top items in the Program Backlog

C) To estimate the size and complexity of the top items in the Program Backlog

D) To identify and address defects and errors in the solution

Answer: B) To refine and elaborate the top items in the Program Backlog

Explanation: The primary goal of Backlog Refinement in SAFe is to refine and elaborate the top items in the Program Backlog, ensuring that the requirements are clear, concise, and ready for development.

Question 172

Which activity occurs during Backlog Refinement in SAFe?

A) Breaking down large features into smaller stories

B) Estimating the size and complexity of the top items in the Program Backlog

C) Prioritizing the Program Backlog based on business value

D) All of the above

Answer: D) All of the above

Explanation: During Backlog Refinement in SAFe, the Development Team and Product Owner collaborate to break down large features into smaller stories, estimate the size and complexity of the top items in the Program Backlog, and prioritize the Program Backlog based on business value.

Question 173

What is the primary benefit of refining the Program Backlog during Backlog Refinement in SAFe?

A) Reduced complexity of the solution

B) Improved estimation accuracy

C) Enhanced collaboration between Development Team and Product Owner

D) Increased speed of development

Answer: C) Enhanced collaboration between Development Team and Product Owner

Explanation: The primary benefit of refining the Program Backlog during Backlog Refinement in SAFe is enhanced collaboration between the Development Team and Product Owner, ensuring that the requirements are clear, concise, and aligned with business objectives.

Question 174

Which of the following is an output of Backlog Refinement in SAFe?

A) A refined and elaborated Program Backlog

B) A prioritized and estimated Program Backlog

C) A detailed design document

D) A test plan

Answer: A) A refined and elaborated Program Backlog

Explanation: The primary output of Backlog Refinement in SAFe is a refined and elaborated Program Backlog, which includes clear, concise, and detailed requirements, ready for development.

Question 175

What is the primary focus of the Development Team during Backlog Refinement in SAFe?

A) Estimating the size and complexity of the top items in the Program Backlog

B) Prioritizing the Program Backlog based on business value

C) Elaborating and refining the requirements for the top items in the Program Backlog

D) Identifying and addressing defects and errors in the solution

Answer: C) Elaborating and refining the requirements for the top items in the Program Backlog

Explanation: The primary focus of the Development Team during Backlog Refinement in SAFe is elaborating and refining the requirements for the top items in the Program Backlog, ensuring that the requirements are clear, concise, and ready for development.

Question 176

Which of the following is a key aspect of Backlog Refinement in SAFe?

A) Ensuring that the Program Backlog is comprehensive and complete

B) Ensuring that the top items in the Program Backlog are estimated and prioritized

C) Ensuring that the Development Team has a clear understanding of the requirements

D) Ensuring that the solution is designed and developed in detail

Answer: C) Ensuring that the Development Team has a clear understanding of the requirements

Explanation: A key aspect of Backlog Refinement in SAFe is ensuring that the Development Team has a clear understanding of the requirements, enabling them to develop the solution effectively and efficiently.

Question 177

What is the primary goal of the Iteration Retrospective in SAFe?

A) To identify and address defects and errors in the solution

B) To improve the processes and practices used by the Agile Release Train (ART)

C) To prioritize and refine the Program Backlog

D) To demonstrate the working solution to stakeholders

Answer: B) To improve the processes and practices used by the Agile Release Train (ART)

Explanation: The primary goal of the Iteration Retrospective in SAFe is to improve the processes and practices used by the Agile Release Train (ART), enabling continuous improvement and increased efficiency.

Question 178

Which of the following is an output of the Iteration Retrospective in SAFe?

A) A list of defects and errors to be addressed

B) A set of action items to improve processes and practices

C) A revised Program Backlog prioritization

D) A detailed design document

Answer: B) A set of action items to improve processes and practices

Explanation: The primary output of the Iteration Retrospective in SAFe is a set of action items to improve processes and practices, which are implemented to increase efficiency and effectiveness of the Agile Release Train (ART).

Question 179

During an Iteration Retrospective in SAFe, what is the primary focus of the "What Went Well" discussion?

A) Identifying and analyzing problems that occurred during the iteration

B) Brainstorming and prioritizing action items for improvement

C) Recognizing and reinforcing positive behaviors and practices

D) Reviewing and refining the Program Backlog

Answer: C) Recognizing and reinforcing positive behaviors and practices

Explanation: The primary focus of the "What Went Well" discussion during an Iteration Retrospective in SAFe is recognizing and reinforcing positive behaviors and practices, to encourage and sustain successful patterns and habits within the Agile Release Train (ART).

QUESTION 180

What is the primary goal of the "Action Items" generated during an Iteration Retrospective in SAFe?

A) To assign blame and responsibility for problems that occurred

B) To document and track defects and errors

C) To implement changes that improve processes and practices

D) To revise and update the Program Backlog

Answer: C) To implement changes that improve processes and practices

Explanation: The primary goal of the "Action Items" generated during an Iteration Retrospective in SAFe is to implement changes that improve processes and practices, enabling the Agile Release Train (ART) to adapt and improve continuously.

PRACTICE TEST - 5

Question 181

During an Iteration Retrospective in SAFe, what is the primary purpose of the "Plus/Delta" exercise?

A) To identify and prioritize defects and errors

B) To brainstorm and generate new ideas for improvement

C) To provide feedback and coaching to team members

D) To reflect on and assess the iteration's processes and practices

Answer: D) To reflect on and assess the iteration's processes and practices

Explanation: The primary purpose of the "Plus/Delta" exercise during an Iteration Retrospective in SAFe is to reflect on and assess the iteration's processes and practices, identifying what worked well (Plus) and what didn't (Delta), to inform improvements.

Question 182

In SAFe, what is the key characteristic of an effective Iteration Retrospective facilitator?

A) Expertise in Agile and SAFe practices

B) Ability to identify and assign action items

C) Skill in leading and managing the team

D) Neutrality and ability to foster open discussion

Answer: D) Neutrality and ability to foster open discussion

Explanation: The key characteristic of an effective Iteration Retrospective facilitator in SAFe is neutrality and the ability to foster open discussion, creating a safe and collaborative environment where team members feel comfortable sharing their thoughts and ideas.

Question 183

During an Iteration Retrospective in SAFe, what is the primary benefit of using a "Retrospective Canvas" or similar visual tool?

A) To provide a structured approach to identifying action items

B) To facilitate open discussion and collaboration among team members

C) To visualize and organize thoughts, ideas, and insights

D) To prioritize and assign tasks to team members

Answer: C) To visualize and organize thoughts, ideas, and insights

Explanation: The primary benefit of using a "Retrospective Canvas" or similar visual tool during an Iteration Retrospective in SAFe is to visualize and organize thoughts, ideas, and insights, enabling the team to better understand and address complex issues.

Question 184

In SAFe, what is the key outcome of an effective Iteration Retrospective?

A) A comprehensive list of defects and errors to be addressed

B) A revised and updated Program Backlog

C) A set of actionable improvements that enhance team processes and practices

D) A detailed plan for implementing changes to the solution

Answer: C) A set of actionable improvements that enhance team processes and practices

Explanation: The key outcome of an effective Iteration Retrospective in SAFe is a set of actionable improvements that enhance team processes and practices, enabling the Agile Release Train (ART) to adapt, learn, and improve continuously.

Question 185

During PI Planning in SAFe, what is the primary purpose of the "Draft Plan Review"?

A) To finalize and approve the Program Increment (PI) plan

B) To review and refine the team's iteration plans

C) To ensure alignment and feasibility of the PI plan

D) To identify and address dependencies between teams

Answer: C) To ensure alignment and feasibility of the PI plan

Explanation: The primary purpose of the "Draft Plan Review" during PI Planning in SAFe is to ensure alignment and feasibility of the PI plan, enabling the Agile Release Train (ART) to commit to a realistic and achievable plan.

Question 186

In SAFe, what is the key benefit of using a "Program Board" during PI Planning?

A) To visualize and track progress during the PI

B) To facilitate communication and collaboration among teams

C) To identify and address dependencies and risks

D) To prioritize and refine the Program Backlog

Answer: C) To identify and address dependencies and risks

Explanation: The key benefit of using a "Program Board" during PI Planning in SAFe is to identify and address dependencies and risks, enabling the Agile Release Train (ART) to develop a cohesive and integrated plan.

Question 187

During PI Planning in SAFe, what is the primary responsibility of the Product Management team?

A) To facilitate the PI Planning event and ensure collaboration among teams

B) To develop and refine the Program Backlog and ensure alignment with business objectives

C) To identify and address technical dependencies and risks

D) To prioritize and refine the team's iteration plans

Answer: B) To develop and refine the Program Backlog and ensure alignment with business objectives

Explanation: The primary responsibility of the Product Management team during PI Planning in SAFe is to develop and refine the Program Backlog and ensure alignment with business objectives, enabling the Agile Release Train (ART) to develop a plan that meets business needs.

Question 188

In SAFe, what is the key outcome of the "Management Review and Problem Solving" activity during PI Planning?

A) A comprehensive list of action items and tasks for the teams

B) A revised and updated Program Backlog

C) A set of resolved dependencies and risks

D) A commitment to the Program Increment (PI) plan

Answer: D) A commitment to the Program Increment (PI) plan

Explanation: The key outcome of the "Management Review and Problem Solving" activity during PI Planning in SAFe is a commitment to the Program Increment (PI) plan, enabling the Agile Release Train (ART) to move forward with a shared understanding and agreement on the plan.

Question 189

During PI Planning in SAFe, what is the primary purpose of the "Team Breakout" sessions?

A) To enable teams to develop their iteration plans and commit to their work

B) To facilitate communication and collaboration among teams

C) To identify and address dependencies and risks

D) To review and refine the Program Backlog

Answer: A) To enable teams to develop their iteration plans and commit to their work

Explanation: The primary purpose of the "Team Breakout" sessions during PI Planning in SAFe is to enable teams to develop their iteration plans and commit to their work, ensuring that each team has a clear understanding of their objectives and responsibilities.

Question 190

In SAFe, what is the key benefit of using a "PI Objectives" document during PI Planning?

A) To provide a detailed description of the solution's architecture

B) To outline the team's iteration plans and commitments

C) To establish a clear understanding of the PI's goals and objectives

D) To identify and address technical dependencies and risks

Answer: C) To establish a clear understanding of the PI's goals and objectives

Explanation: The key benefit of using a "PI Objectives" document during PI Planning in SAFe is to establish a clear understanding of the PI's goals and objectives, enabling the Agile Release Train (ART) to align and focus on the key outcomes to be achieved during the PI.

Question 191

During an IP Iteration in SAFe, what is the primary focus of the Development Teams?

A) To develop and refine the Program Backlog for the next PI

B) To address defects and errors identified during the PI

C) To innovate, experiment, and explore new ideas and technologies

D) To finalize and deploy the solution to production

Answer: C) To innovate, experiment, and explore new ideas and technologies

Explanation: The primary focus of the Development Teams during an IP Iteration in SAFe is to innovate, experiment, and explore new ideas and technologies, enabling the Agile Release Train (ART) to stay ahead of the competition and address emerging trends and opportunities.

Question 192

In SAFe, what is the key benefit of using an IP Iteration to conclude a PI?

A) To ensure that all features and stories are fully developed and tested

B) To provide a buffer for addressing unexpected delays or issues

C) To enable innovation, experimentation, and exploration of new ideas

D) To facilitate knowledge sharing and skill development across teams

Answer: C) To enable innovation, experimentation, and exploration of new ideas

Explanation: The key benefit of using an IP Iteration to conclude a PI in SAFe is to enable innovation, experimentation, and exploration of new ideas, allowing the Agile Release Train (ART) to recharge, refocus, and prepare for the next PI.

Question 193

During an IP Iteration in SAFe, what is the primary responsibility of the Scrum Masters?

A) To facilitate innovation and experimentation activities

B) To ensure that teams are addressing defects and errors

C) To coordinate and facilitate knowledge sharing and skill development

D) To manage and prioritize the Program Backlog

Answer: C) To coordinate and facilitate knowledge sharing and skill development

Explanation: The primary responsibility of the Scrum Masters during an IP Iteration in SAFe is to coordinate and facilitate knowledge sharing and skill development, enabling teams to learn from each other and improve their skills and expertise.

Question 194

In SAFe, what is the key outcome of an IP Iteration?

A) A fully developed and tested solution ready for deployment

B) A refined and updated Program Backlog for the next PI

C) A set of innovative solutions and prototypes to inform future development

D) A team of skilled and knowledgeable professionals ready for the next PI

Answer: C) A set of innovative solutions and prototypes to inform future development

Explanation: The key outcome of an IP Iteration in SAFe is a set of innovative solutions and prototypes to inform future development, enabling the Agile Release Train (ART) to explore new ideas, technologies, and approaches that can drive future success.

Question 195

During an IP Iteration in SAFe, what is the primary focus of the System Demo?

A) To showcase the fully developed and tested solution to stakeholders

B) To demonstrate innovative solutions and prototypes to inform future development

C) To review and refine the Program Backlog for the next PI

D) To facilitate knowledge sharing and skill development across teams

Answer: B) To demonstrate innovative solutions and prototypes to inform future development

Explanation: The primary focus of the System Demo during an IP Iteration in SAFe is to demonstrate innovative solutions and prototypes to inform future development, enabling stakeholders to see the innovative work done during the IP Iteration.

Question 196

In SAFe, what is the key benefit of using an IP Iteration to conclude a PI?

A) To ensure that all features and stories are fully developed and tested

B) To provide a buffer for addressing unexpected delays or issues

C) To enable teams to recharge and refocus before the next PI

D) To facilitate alignment and planning for the next PI

Answer: C) To enable teams to recharge and refocus before the next PI

Explanation: The key benefit of using an IP Iteration to conclude a PI in SAFe is to enable teams to recharge and refocus before the next PI, allowing them to take a break from the intense PI schedule and come back refreshed and ready for the next PI.

Question 197

During the Inspect and Adapt event in SAFe, what is the primary focus of the "Problem Solving" activity?

A) To identify and prioritize defects and errors

B) To develop and implement solutions to systemic problems

C) To review and refine the Program Backlog

D) To facilitate knowledge sharing and skill development

Answer: B) To develop and implement solutions to systemic problems

Explanation: The primary focus of the "Problem Solving" activity during the Inspect and Adapt event in SAFe is to develop and implement solutions to systemic problems, enabling the Agile Release Train (ART) to address underlying issues and improve overall performance.

Question 198

In SAFe, what is the key outcome of the "Solution Demo" during the Inspect and Adapt event?

A) A comprehensive list of defects and errors to be addressed

B) A set of actionable improvements to address systemic problems

C) A refined and updated Program Backlog

D) A demonstration of the fully developed and tested solution

Answer: B) A set of actionable improvements to address systemic problems

Explanation: The key outcome of the "Solution Demo" during the Inspect and Adapt event in SAFe is a set of actionable improvements to address systemic problems, enabling the Agile Release Train (ART) to identify and implement solutions to improve overall performance and delivery.

Question 199

During the Inspect and Adapt event in SAFe, what is the primary responsibility of the Scrum Masters?

A) To facilitate the Solution Demo and review of the solution

B) To lead the problem-solving activities and identify solutions

C) To ensure that the event is conducted in accordance with SAFe principles

D) To facilitate collaboration and communication among teams

Answer: C) To ensure that the event is conducted in accordance with SAFe principles

Explanation: The primary responsibility of the Scrum Masters during the Inspect and Adapt event in SAFe is to ensure that the event is conducted in accordance with SAFe principles, enabling a smooth and effective event that drives meaningful improvement.

Question 200

In SAFe, what is the key benefit of using a "Metrics and Trends" report during the Inspect and Adapt event?

A) To identify and prioritize defects and errors

B) To track progress and performance over time

C) To facilitate knowledge sharing and skill development

D) To review and refine the Program Backlog

Answer: B) To track progress and performance over time

Explanation: The key benefit of using a "Metrics and Trends" report during the Inspect and Adapt event in SAFe is to track progress and performance over time, enabling the Agile Release Train (ART) to understand trends, identify areas for improvement, and make data-driven decisions.

Question 201

During the Inspect and Adapt event in SAFe, what is the primary focus of the "Retrospective" activity?

A) To review and refine the Program Backlog

B) To identify and prioritize defects and errors

C) To reflect on and improve the Agile Release Train's processes and practices

D) To facilitate knowledge sharing and skill development

Answer: C) To reflect on and improve the Agile Release Train's processes and practices

Explanation: The primary focus of the "Retrospective" activity during the Inspect and Adapt event in SAFe is to reflect on and improve the Agile Release Train's processes and practices, enabling the ART to identify areas for improvement and implement changes to increase efficiency and effectiveness.

Question 202

In SAFe, what is the key outcome of the "Action Item Review" during the Inspect and Adapt event?

A) A comprehensive list of defects and errors to be addressed

B) A set of actionable improvements to address systemic problems

C) A refined and updated Program Backlog

D) A list of assigned action items with clear owners and due dates

Answer: D) A list of assigned action items with clear owners and due dates

Explanation: The key outcome of the "Action Item Review" during the Inspect and Adapt event in SAFe is a list of assigned action items with clear owners and due dates, ensuring that identified improvements are implemented and tracked to increase the Agile Release Train's performance and delivery.

Question 203

During the Inspect and Adapt event in SAFe, what is the primary role of the Agile Release Train (ART) stakeholders?

A) To provide input on the Program Backlog and priorities

B) To review and approve the solution and action items

C) To participate in problem-solving and improvement activities

D) To observe and learn from the event

Answer: C) To participate in problem-solving and improvement activities

Explanation: The primary role of the Agile Release Train (ART) stakeholders during the Inspect and Adapt event in SAFe is to participate in problem-solving and improvement activities, enabling collaborative and inclusive decision-making to drive meaningful change.

Question 204

In SAFe, what is the key benefit of using a "Solution Canvas" during the Inspect and Adapt event?

A) To visualize and organize defects and errors

B) To facilitate communication and collaboration among teams

C) To identify and address systemic problems and opportunities

D) To review and refine the Program Backlog

Answer: C) To identify and address systemic problems and opportunities

Explanation: The key benefit of using a "Solution Canvas" during the Inspect and Adapt event in SAFe is to identify and address systemic problems and opportunities, enabling the Agile Release Train (ART) to visualize and tackle complex issues and drive holistic improvement.

Question 205

In a SAFe enterprise, what is the primary responsibility of Agile Teams in regards to alignment?

A) To ensure alignment with the company's vision and strategy

B) To align with the Program Increment (PI) objectives and goals

C) To align with the team's iteration goals and objectives

D) To align with the individual's goals and objectives

Answer: B) To align with the Program Increment (PI) objectives and goals

Explanation: The primary responsibility of Agile Teams in a SAFe enterprise is to align with the Program Increment (PI) objectives and goals, ensuring that their work is focused on delivering value that meets the ART's and enterprise's objectives.

Question 206

In SAFe, what is the key benefit of Agile Teams using a "Definition of Done" (DoD)?

A) To ensure that all work is completed to a high standard

B) To facilitate communication and collaboration among teams

C) To provide a clear understanding of quality and completeness

D) To enable teams to work independently without oversight

Answer: C) To provide a clear understanding of quality and completeness

Explanation: The key benefit of Agile Teams using a "Definition of Done" (DoD) in SAFe is to provide a clear understanding of quality and completeness, ensuring that all work meets the same standards and is delivered with consistency and reliability.

Question 207

A SAFe enterprise is experiencing delays in delivering value to customers due to dependencies between teams. What should the Agile Teams do to address this issue?

A) Work on their own iteration goals and objectives without considering dependencies

B) Collaborate with other teams to identify and address dependencies

C) Focus on completing their own work and let other teams handle their dependencies

D) Escalate the issue to management to resolve

Answer: B) Collaborate with other teams to identify and address dependencies

Explanation: In a SAFe enterprise, Agile Teams should collaborate with other teams to identify and address dependencies, ensuring that they work together to deliver value to customers. This requires communication, coordination, and cooperation among teams.

Question 208

An Agile Team in a SAFe enterprise is struggling to meet its iteration goals due to lack of skills and expertise. What should the team do to address this issue?

A) Ask management to provide additional training and resources

B) Hire new team members with the required skills and expertise

C) Collaborate with other teams to share knowledge and skills

D) Reduce the iteration goals and objectives to make them more achievable

Answer: C) Collaborate with other teams to share knowledge and skills

Explanation: In a SAFe enterprise, Agile Teams should collaborate with other teams to share knowledge and skills, enabling them to leverage the expertise and experience of other teams to address skill gaps and improve overall performance.

Question 209

A SAFe enterprise is implementing a new technology that requires significant changes to the existing architecture. How should the Agile Teams approach this change?

A) Continue with their current iteration goals and objectives, ignoring the architectural changes

B) Pause their current work and focus on implementing the new technology

C) Collaborate with the architecture team to understand the changes and adapt their work accordingly

D) Resist the change and argue that it's not necessary

Answer: C) Collaborate with the architecture team to understand the changes and adapt their work accordingly

Explanation: In a SAFe enterprise, Agile Teams should collaborate with the architecture team to understand the changes and adapt their work accordingly, ensuring that they can effectively implement the new technology and deliver value to customers.

Question 210

An Agile Team in a SAFe enterprise is experiencing high turnover, with several team members leaving the team in a short period. How should the team handle this situation?

A) Focus on completing the current iteration and worry about the turnover later

B) Pause the current work and focus on rebuilding the team

C) Collaborate with other teams to share knowledge and skills and minimize the impact of the turnover

D) Ask management to provide additional resources to replace the leaving team members

Answer: C) Collaborate with other teams to share knowledge and skills and minimize the impact of the turnover

Explanation: In a SAFe enterprise, Agile Teams should collaborate with other teams to share knowledge and skills and minimize the impact of the turnover, ensuring that they can continue to deliver value to customers despite the changes in team membership.

Question 211

A SAFe enterprise is experiencing conflicting priorities between different stakeholders, leading to confusion and delays. How should the Agile Teams handle this situation?

A) Prioritize the needs of the most vocal stakeholder

B) Focus on delivering the highest business value, regardless of stakeholder priorities

C) Collaborate with stakeholders to understand and reconcile conflicting priorities

D) Escalate the issue to management to resolve

Answer: C) Collaborate with stakeholders to understand and reconcile conflicting priorities

Explanation: In a SAFe enterprise, Agile Teams should collaborate with stakeholders to understand and reconcile conflicting priorities, ensuring that everyone is aligned and working towards the same goals.

Question 212

An Agile Team in a SAFe enterprise is struggling to meet its commitments due to unrealistic expectations from stakeholders. How should the team handle this situation?

A) Accept the unrealistic expectations and try to deliver

B) Push back on the stakeholders and refuse to accept the commitments

C) Collaborate with stakeholders to understand their needs and negotiate realistic commitments

D) Ask management to intervene and resolve the issue

Answer: C) Collaborate with stakeholders to understand their needs and negotiate realistic commitments

Explanation: In a SAFe enterprise, Agile Teams should collaborate with stakeholders to understand their needs and negotiate realistic commitments, ensuring that everyone has a shared understanding of what can be delivered and when.

Question 213

A SAFe enterprise is undergoing a significant organizational restructuring, resulting in changes to team compositions and roles. How should the Agile Teams adapt to this situation?

A) Continue with their current work and ignore the changes

B) Pause their work and wait for the restructuring to complete

C) Collaborate with other teams and stakeholders to understand the changes and adapt their processes and workflows

D) Resist the changes and argue that they are unnecessary

Answer: C) Collaborate with other teams and stakeholders to understand the changes and adapt their processes and workflows

Explanation: In a SAFe enterprise, Agile Teams should collaborate with other teams and stakeholders to understand the changes and adapt their processes and workflows, ensuring that they can continue to deliver value to customers despite the organizational changes.

Question 214

An Agile Team in a SAFe enterprise is experiencing a significant increase in technical debt due to rapid changes in market conditions. How should the team handle this situation?

A) Ignore the technical debt and focus on delivering new features

B) Pause their work and focus on paying down the technical debt

C) Collaborate with stakeholders to understand the trade-offs between technical debt and new features

D) Ask management to provide additional resources to address the technical debt

Answer: C) Collaborate with stakeholders to understand the trade-offs between technical debt and new features

Explanation: In a SAFe enterprise, Agile Teams should collaborate with stakeholders to understand the trade-offs between technical debt and new features, ensuring that they can make informed decisions about how to balance short-term delivery with long-term sustainability.

Question 215

A SAFe enterprise is experiencing a high rate of defects and errors in production, leading to customer dissatisfaction. How should the Agile Teams address this situation?

A) Focus on increasing velocity to deliver more features

B) Implement additional testing and quality assurance measures

C) Collaborate with stakeholders to understand root causes and implement corrective actions

D) Blame the quality assurance team for not catching the defects

Answer: C) Collaborate with stakeholders to understand root causes and implement corrective actions

Explanation: In a SAFe enterprise, Agile Teams should collaborate with stakeholders to understand root causes and implement corrective actions, ensuring that they address the underlying issues leading to defects and errors.

Question 216

An Agile Team in a SAFe enterprise is struggling to integrate with a newly acquired company, leading to cultural and process clashes. How should the team handle this situation?

A) Impose their own processes and culture on the newly acquired company

B) Ignore the cultural and process differences and focus on delivering results

C) Collaborate with the newly acquired company to understand their processes and culture

D) Ask management to intervene and resolve the issues

Answer: C) Collaborate with the newly acquired company to understand their processes and culture

Explanation: In a SAFe enterprise, Agile Teams should collaborate with the newly acquired company to understand their processes and culture, ensuring that they can find common ground and integrate effectively to deliver value to customers.

Question 217

A SAFe enterprise is experiencing a significant delay in delivering a critical feature due to a dependent team's lack of progress. How should the Agile Teams address this situation?

A) Work around the dependent team's delay by implementing a temporary solution

B) Escalate the issue to management to resolve

C) Collaborate with the dependent team to understand the root cause and develop a recovery plan

D) Reduce the scope of the feature to exclude the dependent team's work

Answer: C) Collaborate with the dependent team to understand the root cause and develop a recovery plan

Explanation: In a SAFe enterprise, Agile Teams should collaborate with the dependent team to understand the root cause and develop a recovery plan, ensuring that they can work together to get the feature back on track.

Question 218

An Agile Team in a SAFe enterprise is struggling to adopt a new technology due to lack of expertise and resources. How should the team handle this situation?

A) Ask management to provide additional training and resources

B) Hire external consultants to implement the technology

C) Collaborate with other teams to share knowledge and expertise

D) Postpone the adoption of the new technology until later

Answer: C) Collaborate with other teams to share knowledge and expertise

Explanation: In a SAFe enterprise, Agile Teams should collaborate with other teams to share knowledge and expertise, ensuring that they can leverage the collective knowledge of the organization to overcome technical challenges.

Question 219

A SAFe enterprise is experiencing a high rate of turnover among Agile Team members, leading to knowledge gaps and decreased productivity. How should the Agile Teams address this situation?

A) Focus on documenting knowledge and processes to mitigate the impact of turnover

B) Implement a rigorous training program to quickly onboard new team members

C) Collaborate with other teams to share knowledge and expertise

D) Reduce the scope of work to accommodate the reduced team capacity

Answer: C) Collaborate with other teams to share knowledge and expertise

Explanation: In a SAFe enterprise, Agile Teams should collaborate with other teams to share knowledge and expertise, ensuring that they can leverage the collective knowledge of the organization to overcome the challenges posed by high turnover.

Question 220

An Agile Team in a SAFe enterprise is struggling to balance the needs of multiple stakeholders with competing priorities. How should the team handle this situation?

A) Prioritize the needs of the most vocal stakeholder

B) Focus on delivering the highest business value, regardless of stakeholder priorities

C) Collaborate with stakeholders to understand and reconcile competing priorities

D) Ask management to intervene and resolve the conflicts

Answer: C) Collaborate with stakeholders to understand and reconcile competing priorities

Explanation: In a SAFe enterprise, Agile Teams should collaborate with stakeholders to understand and reconcile competing priorities, ensuring that they can deliver value to customers while meeting the needs of multiple stakeholders.

Question 221

A SAFe enterprise is experiencing a significant increase in technical debt due to rapid experimentation and innovation. How should the Agile Teams address this situation?

A) Prioritize paying down technical debt over delivering new features

B) Implement a "tech debt budget" to allocate resources for debt reduction

C) Collaborate with stakeholders to understand the trade-offs between technical debt and innovation

D) Ignore the technical debt and focus on delivering new features

Answer: C) Collaborate with stakeholders to understand the trade-offs between technical debt and innovation

Explanation: In a SAFe enterprise, Agile Teams should collaborate with stakeholders to understand the trade-offs between technical debt and innovation, ensuring that they can make informed decisions about how to balance short-term innovation with long-term sustainability.

Question 222

An Agile Team in a SAFe enterprise is struggling to integrate with a third-party vendor, leading to delays and quality issues. How should the team handle this situation?

A) Take ownership of the vendor's work and implement it themselves

B) Collaborate with the vendor to understand their processes and improve integration

C) Escalate the issue to management to resolve

D) Reduce the scope of work to exclude the vendor's components

Answer: B) Collaborate with the vendor to understand their processes and improve integration

Explanation: In a SAFe enterprise, Agile Teams should collaborate with the vendor to understand their processes and improve integration, ensuring that they can work together effectively to deliver value to customers.

Question 223

A SAFe enterprise is experiencing a cultural clash between Agile Teams and traditional project management teams, leading to conflicts and delays. How should the Agile Teams address this situation?

A) Implement Agile practices and principles across the entire organization

B) Collaborate with traditional project management teams to understand their concerns and find common ground

C) Focus on delivering results and ignore the cultural differences

D) Ask management to intervene and resolve the conflicts

Answer: B) Collaborate with traditional project management teams to understand their concerns and find common ground

Explanation: In a SAFe enterprise, Agile Teams should collaborate with traditional project management teams to understand their concerns and find common ground, ensuring that they can work together effectively to deliver value to customers.

Question 224

An Agile Team in a SAFe enterprise is struggling to prioritize features due to conflicting stakeholder demands and limited resources. How should the team handle this situation?

A) Prioritize features based on business value and customer needs

B) Use a "first-come, first-served" approach to prioritize features

C) Collaborate with stakeholders to understand their needs and negotiate priorities

D) Ask management to prioritize features and allocate resources

Answer: C) Collaborate with stakeholders to understand their needs and negotiate priorities

Explanation: In a SAFe enterprise, Agile Teams should collaborate with stakeholders to understand their needs and negotiate priorities, ensuring that they can deliver value to customers while meeting the needs of multiple stakeholders.

Question 225

A SAFe enterprise is experiencing a significant increase in cybersecurity threats, requiring Agile Teams to implement additional security measures. How should the teams handle this situation?

A) Prioritize security measures over delivering new features

B) Implement security measures in a separate iteration to avoid impacting delivery

C) Collaborate with cybersecurity experts to understand threats and implement mitigations

D) Ignore security measures and focus on delivering new features

Answer: C) Collaborate with cybersecurity experts to understand threats and implement mitigations

Explanation: In a SAFe enterprise, Agile Teams should collaborate with cybersecurity experts to understand threats and implement mitigations, ensuring that they can deliver secure solutions to customers.

PRACTICE TEST - 6

Question 226

An Agile Team in a SAFe enterprise is struggling to maintain a consistent velocity due to frequent changes in team composition and availability. How should the team handle this situation?

A) Adjust iteration goals based on changing team availability

B) Focus on delivering high-priority features regardless of velocity

C) Collaborate with other teams to share resources and expertise

D) Ask management to provide additional resources to stabilize the team

Answer: C) Collaborate with other teams to share resources and expertise

Explanation: In a SAFe enterprise, Agile Teams should collaborate with other teams to share resources and expertise, ensuring that they can maintain a consistent velocity and deliver value to customers despite changes in team composition and availability.

Question 227

A SAFe enterprise is experiencing a high rate of defects in production due to inadequate testing practices. How should the Agile Teams address this situation?

A) Implement additional testing iterations to ensure thorough testing

B) Collaborate with testing teams to develop and implement comprehensive testing strategies

C) Focus on delivering new features and ignore testing concerns

D) Ask management to provide additional resources for testing

Answer: B) Collaborate with testing teams to develop and implement comprehensive testing strategies

Explanation: In a SAFe enterprise, Agile Teams should collaborate with testing teams to develop and implement comprehensive testing strategies, ensuring that they can deliver high-quality solutions to customers.

Question 228

An Agile Team in a SAFe enterprise is struggling to balance the needs of multiple stakeholders with competing priorities and limited resources. How should the team handle this situation?

A) Prioritize stakeholders based on business value and customer needs

B) Use a "first-come, first-served" approach to prioritize stakeholders

C) Collaborate with stakeholders to understand their needs and negotiate priorities

D) Ask management to prioritize stakeholders and allocate resources

Answer: C) Collaborate with stakeholders to understand their needs and negotiate priorities

Explanation: In a SAFe enterprise, Agile Teams should collaborate with stakeholders to understand their needs and negotiate priorities, ensuring that they can deliver value to customers while meeting the needs of multiple stakeholders.

Question 229

A SAFe enterprise is implementing a microservices architecture, and Agile Teams are struggling to manage dependencies between services. How should the teams handle this situation?

A) Use a centralized integration team to manage dependencies

B) Implement a "publish and subscribe" model for service integration

C) Collaborate with other teams to develop and implement a service integration framework

D) Use a monolithic architecture to avoid dependency issues

Answer: C) Collaborate with other teams to develop and implement a service integration framework

Explanation: In a SAFe enterprise, Agile Teams should collaborate with other teams to develop and implement a service integration framework, ensuring that they can manage dependencies effectively and deliver a cohesive solution.

Question 230

An Agile Team in a SAFe enterprise is experiencing issues with their continuous integration/continuous deployment (CI/CD) pipeline, leading to delays in delivering value to customers. How should the team handle this situation?

A) Implement a manual testing phase to ensure quality

B) Use a "big bang" approach to deploy all changes at once

C) Collaborate with DevOps teams to identify and resolve pipeline issues

D) Reduce the frequency of deployments to reduce pipeline stress

Answer: C) Collaborate with DevOps teams to identify and resolve pipeline issues

Explanation: In a SAFe enterprise, Agile Teams should collaborate with DevOps teams to identify and resolve pipeline issues, ensuring that they can deliver value to customers quickly and reliably.

Question 231

A SAFe enterprise is adopting a cloud-native architecture, and Agile Teams are struggling to manage containerization and orchestration. How should the teams handle this situation?

A) Use a single containerization platform for all services

B) Implement a centralized orchestration team to manage containerization

C) Collaborate with other teams to develop and implement a containerization and orchestration framework

D) Use a virtual machine-based approach to avoid containerization issues

Answer: C) Collaborate with other teams to develop and implement a containerization and orchestration framework

Explanation: In a SAFe enterprise, Agile Teams should collaborate with other teams to develop and implement a containerization and orchestration framework, ensuring that they can manage containerization and orchestration effectively and deliver a cohesive solution.

Question 232

An Agile Team in a SAFe enterprise is experiencing issues with their test automation framework, leading to delays in testing and delivery. How should the team handle this situation?

A) Implement a manual testing approach to supplement automation

B) Use a "record and playback" approach to automate testing

C) Collaborate with other teams to develop and implement a comprehensive test automation framework

D) Reduce the scope of testing to reduce automation stress

Answer: C) Collaborate with other teams to develop and implement a comprehensive test automation framework

Explanation: In a SAFe enterprise, Agile Teams should collaborate with other teams to develop and implement a comprehensive test automation framework, ensuring that they can deliver high-quality solutions quickly and reliably.

Question 233

A SAFe enterprise is implementing a DevOps culture, and Agile Teams are struggling to integrate security practices into their workflows. How should the teams handle this situation?

A) Implement a separate security team to handle security concerns

B) Use a "shift left" approach to integrate security practices into development workflows

C) Collaborate with security teams to develop and implement a comprehensive security framework

D) Reduce the scope of security practices to reduce integration stress

Answer: B) Use a "shift left" approach to integrate security practices into development workflows

Explanation: In a SAFe enterprise, Agile Teams should use a "shift left" approach to integrate security practices into development workflows, ensuring that they can deliver secure solutions quickly and reliably.

Question 234

An Agile Team in a SAFe enterprise is experiencing issues with their data analytics and visualization capabilities, leading to poor decision-making. How should the team handle this situation?

A) Implement a separate data analytics team to handle data concerns

B) Use a "data lake" approach to store and analyze data

C) Collaborate with data analytics teams to develop and implement a comprehensive data analytics framework

D) Reduce the scope of data analytics to reduce complexity

Answer: C) Collaborate with data analytics teams to develop and implement a comprehensive data analytics framework

Explanation: In a SAFe enterprise, Agile Teams should collaborate with data analytics teams to develop and implement a comprehensive data analytics framework, ensuring that they can make informed decisions quickly and reliably.

Question 235

A SAFe enterprise is adopting a serverless architecture, and Agile Teams are struggling to manage event-driven design and asynchronous processing. How should the teams handle this situation?

A) Implement a centralized event management team to handle event-driven design

B) Use a "request-response" approach to simplify asynchronous processing

C) Collaborate with other teams to develop and implement an event-driven architecture framework

D) Reduce the scope of serverless adoption to reduce complexity

Answer: C) Collaborate with other teams to develop and implement an event-driven architecture framework

Explanation: In a SAFe enterprise, Agile Teams should collaborate with other teams to develop and implement an event-driven architecture framework, ensuring that they can manage event-driven design and asynchronous processing effectively.

Question 236

An Agile Team in a SAFe enterprise is experiencing issues with their artificial intelligence (AI) and machine learning (ML) model development, leading to poor model accuracy. How should the team handle this situation?

A) Implement a separate AI/ML team to handle model development

B) Use a "black box" approach to AI/ML model development

C) Collaborate with data science teams to develop and implement a comprehensive AI/ML framework

D) Reduce the scope of AI/ML adoption to reduce complexity

Answer: C) Collaborate with data science teams to develop and implement a comprehensive AI/ML framework

Explanation: In a SAFe enterprise, Agile Teams should collaborate with data science teams to develop and implement a comprehensive AI/ML framework, ensuring that they can deliver accurate and reliable AI/ML models.

Question 237

A SAFe enterprise is implementing a Kubernetes-based container orchestration platform, and Agile Teams are struggling to manage pod scaling and resource allocation. How should the teams handle this situation?

A) Implement a horizontal pod autoscaler (HPA) to dynamically scale pods

B) Use a resource quota to limit pod resource allocation

C) Collaborate with platform teams to develop and implement a comprehensive Kubernetes resource management framework

D) Reduce the scope of Kubernetes adoption to reduce complexity

Answer: C) Collaborate with platform teams to develop and implement a comprehensive Kubernetes resource management framework

Explanation: In a SAFe enterprise, Agile Teams should collaborate with platform teams to develop and implement a comprehensive Kubernetes resource management framework, ensuring that they can effectively manage pod scaling and resource allocation.

Question 238

An Agile Team in a SAFe enterprise is experiencing issues with their Apache Kafka-based event streaming architecture, leading to poor event processing throughput. How should the team handle this situation?

A) Implement a Kafka topic partitioning strategy to improve event processing throughput

B) Use a Kafka consumer group to balance event processing load

C) Collaborate with data engineering teams to develop and implement a comprehensive event streaming framework

D) Reduce the scope of Kafka adoption to reduce complexity

Answer: C) Collaborate with data engineering teams to develop and implement a comprehensive event streaming framework

Explanation: In a SAFe enterprise, Agile Teams should collaborate with data engineering teams to develop and implement a comprehensive event streaming framework, ensuring that they can deliver high-throughput event processing capabilities.

Question 239

A SAFe enterprise is implementing a service mesh architecture using Istio, and Agile Teams are struggling to manage service discovery and traffic management. How should the teams handle this situation?

A) Implement an Istio ingress gateway to manage incoming traffic

B) Use an Istio sidecar proxy to manage service discovery and traffic management

C) Collaborate with platform teams to develop and implement a comprehensive service mesh framework

D) Reduce the scope of Istio adoption to reduce complexity

Answer: C) Collaborate with platform teams to develop and implement a comprehensive service mesh framework

Explanation: In a SAFe enterprise, Agile Teams should collaborate with platform teams to develop and implement a comprehensive service mesh framework, ensuring that they can effectively manage service discovery and traffic management.

Question 240

An Agile Team in a SAFe enterprise is experiencing issues with their GraphQL-based API gateway, leading to poor query performance and complexity. How should the team handle this situation?

A) Implement a GraphQL schema stitching strategy to improve query performance

B) Use a GraphQL resolver to optimize query complexity

C) Collaborate with API teams to develop and implement a comprehensive API gateway framework

D) Reduce the scope of GraphQL adoption to reduce complexity

Answer: C) Collaborate with API teams to develop and implement a comprehensive API gateway framework

Explanation: In a SAFe enterprise, Agile Teams should collaborate with API teams to develop and implement a comprehensive API gateway framework, ensuring that they can deliver high-performance and scalable APIs.

Question 241

A SAFe enterprise is implementing a cloud-native architecture using AWS Lambda, and Agile Teams are struggling to manage serverless function concurrency and error handling. How should the teams handle this situation?

A) Implement an AWS Lambda destination function to handle errors

B) Use an AWS Lambda concurrency limit to manage function concurrency

C) Collaborate with DevOps teams to develop and implement a comprehensive serverless framework

D) Reduce the scope of AWS Lambda adoption to reduce complexity

Answer: C) Collaborate with DevOps teams to develop and implement a comprehensive serverless framework

Explanation: In a SAFe enterprise, Agile Teams should collaborate with DevOps teams to develop and implement a comprehensive serverless framework, ensuring that they can effectively manage serverless function concurrency and error handling.

Question 242

An Agile Team in a SAFe enterprise is experiencing issues with their Terraform-based infrastructure as code (IaC) implementation, leading to poor infrastructure provisioning and management. How should the team handle this situation?

A) Implement a Terraform module to standardize infrastructure provisioning

B) Use a Terraform state file to manage infrastructure configuration

C) Collaborate with DevOps teams to develop and implement a comprehensive IaC framework

D) Reduce the scope of Terraform adoption to reduce complexity

Answer: C) Collaborate with DevOps teams to develop and implement a comprehensive IaC framework

Explanation: In a SAFe enterprise, Agile Teams should collaborate with DevOps teams to develop and implement a comprehensive IaC framework, ensuring that they can deliver consistent and reliable infrastructure provisioning and management.

Question 243

A SAFe enterprise is implementing a microservices architecture using Docker containers, and Agile Teams are struggling to manage container networking and service discovery. How should the teams handle this situation?

A) Implement a Docker overlay network to manage container networking

B) Use a Docker registry to manage container images and service discovery

C) Collaborate with DevOps teams to develop and implement a comprehensive container orchestration framework

D) Reduce the scope of Docker adoption to reduce complexity

Answer: C) Collaborate with DevOps teams to develop and implement a comprchensive container orchestration framework

Explanation: In a SAFe enterprise, Agile Teams should collaborate with DevOps teams to develop and implement a comprehensive container orchestration framework, ensuring that they can effectively manage container networking and service discovery.

Question 244

An Agile Team in a SAFe enterprise is experiencing issues with their Apache Cassandra-based NoSQL database, leading to poor data consistency and scalability. How should the team handle this situation?

A) Implement an Apache Cassandra cluster to improve data scalability

B) Use an Apache Cassandra materialized view to improve data consistency

C) Collaborate with data engineering teams to develop and implement a comprehensive NoSQL database framework

D) Reduce the scope of Apache Cassandra adoption to reduce complexity

Answer: C) Collaborate with data engineering teams to develop and implement a comprehensive NoSQL database framework

Explanation: In a SAFe enterprise, Agile Teams should collaborate with data engineering teams to develop and implement a comprehensive NoSQL database framework, ensuring that they can deliver high-performance and scalable data storage solutions.

Question 245

A SAFe enterprise is implementing a continuous delivery pipeline using Jenkins, and Agile Teams are struggling to manage pipeline complexity and scalability. How should the teams handle this situation?

A) Implement a Jenkins pipeline as code to manage pipeline complexity

B) Use a Jenkins shared library to manage pipeline scalability

C) Collaborate with DevOps teams to develop and implement a comprehensive continuous delivery framework

D) Reduce the scope of Jenkins adoption to reduce complexity

Answer: C) Collaborate with DevOps teams to develop and implement a comprehensive continuous delivery framework

Explanation: In a SAFe enterprise, Agile Teams should collaborate with DevOps teams to develop and implement a comprehensive continuous delivery framework, ensuring that they can effectively manage pipeline complexity and scalability.

Question 246

An Agile Team in a SAFe enterprise is experiencing issues with their Elasticsearch-based search and analytics implementation, leading to poor search performance and data accuracy. How should the team handle this situation?

A) Implement an Elasticsearch index template to improve search performance

B) Use an Elasticsearch data pipeline to improve data accuracy

C) Collaborate with data engineering teams to develop and implement a comprehensive search and analytics framework

D) Reduce the scope of Elasticsearch adoption to reduce complexity

Answer: C) Collaborate with data engineering teams to develop and implement a comprehensive search and analytics framework

Explanation: In a SAFe enterprise, Agile Teams should collaborate with data engineering teams to develop and implement a comprehensive search and analytics framework, ensuring that they can deliver high-performance and accurate search and analytics capabilities.

Question 247

A SAFe enterprise is implementing a cloud-native architecture using Azure Kubernetes Service (AKS), and Agile Teams are struggling to manage cluster security and compliance. How should the teams handle this situation?

A) Implement Azure Active Directory (AAD) integration with AKS to manage cluster security

B) Use Azure Policy to manage cluster compliance

C) Collaborate with DevOps teams to develop and implement a comprehensive cloud-native security framework

D) Reduce the scope of AKS adoption to reduce complexity

Answer: C) Collaborate with DevOps teams to develop and implement a comprehensive cloud-native security framework

Explanation: In a SAFe enterprise, Agile Teams should collaborate with DevOps teams to develop and implement a comprehensive cloud-native security framework, ensuring that they can effectively manage cluster security and compliance.

Question 248

An Agile Team in a SAFe enterprise is experiencing issues with their Apache Kafka-based event-driven architecture, leading to poor event processing reliability and scalability. How should the team handle this situation?

A) Implement Kafka topic replication to improve event processing reliability

B) Use Kafka consumer groups to improve event processing scalability

C) Collaborate with data engineering teams to develop and implement a comprehensive event-driven architecture framework

D) Reduce the scope of Kafka adoption to reduce complexity

Answer: C) Collaborate with data engineering teams to develop and implement a comprehensive event-driven architecture framework

Explanation: In a SAFe enterprise, Agile Teams should collaborate with data engineering teams to develop and implement a comprehensive event-driven architecture framework, ensuring that they can deliver high-reliability and scalable event processing capabilities.

Question 249

A SAFe enterprise is implementing a microservices architecture using gRPC, and Agile Teams are struggling to manage service discovery and communication. How should the teams handle this situation?

A) Implement a gRPC service registry to manage service discovery

B) Use gRPC metadata to manage service communication

C) Collaborate with DevOps teams to develop and implement a comprehensive microservices communication framework

D) Reduce the scope of gRPC adoption to reduce complexity

Answer: C) Collaborate with DevOps teams to develop and implement a comprehensive microservices communication framework

Explanation: In a SAFe enterprise, Agile Teams should collaborate with DevOps teams to develop and implement a comprehensive microservices communication framework, ensuring that they can effectively manage service discovery and communication.

Question 250

An Agile Team in a SAFe enterprise is experiencing issues with their MongoDB-based NoSQL database, leading to poor data consistency and performance. How should the team handle this situation?

A) Implement MongoDB transactions to improve data consistency

B) Use MongoDB indexing to improve query performance

C) Collaborate with data engineering teams to develop and implement a comprehensive NoSQL database optimization framework

D) Reduce the scope of MongoDB adoption to reduce complexity

Answer: C) Collaborate with data engineering teams to develop and implement a comprehensive NoSQL database optimization framework

Explanation: In a SAFe enterprise, Agile Teams should collaborate with data engineering teams to develop and implement a comprehensive NoSQL database optimization framework, ensuring that they can deliver high-performance and consistent data storage solutions.

Question 251

A SAFe enterprise is implementing a DevOps pipeline using GitLab CI/CD, and Agile Teams are struggling to manage pipeline complexity and scalability. How should the teams handle this situation?

A) Implement a GitLab CI/CD child pipeline to manage pipeline complexity

B) Use a GitLab CI/CD environment to manage pipeline scalability

C) Collaborate with DevOps teams to develop and implement a comprehensive DevOps pipeline framework

D) Reduce the scope of GitLab CI/CD adoption to reduce complexity

Answer: C) Collaborate with DevOps teams to develop and implement a comprehensive DevOps pipeline framework

Explanation: In a SAFe enterprise, Agile Teams should collaborate with DevOps teams to develop and implement a comprehensive DevOps pipeline framework, ensuring that they can effectively manage pipeline complexity and scalability.

Question 252

An Agile Team in a SAFe enterprise is experiencing issues with their Apache Spark-based data processing implementation, leading to poor data processing performance and scalability. How should the team handle this situation?

A) Implement Apache Spark data partitioning to improve data processing performance

B) Use Apache Spark caching to improve data processing scalability

C) Collaborate with data engineering teams to develop and implement a comprehensive data processing optimization framework

D) Reduce the scope of Apache Spark adoption to reduce complexity

Answer: C) Collaborate with data engineering teams to develop and implement a comprehensive data processing optimization framework

Explanation: In a SAFe enterprise, Agile Teams should collaborate with data engineering teams to develop and implement a comprehensive data processing optimization framework, ensuring that they can deliver high-performance and scalable data processing capabilities.

Question 253

A SAFe enterprise is implementing a containerized application using Docker and Kubernetes, and Agile Teams are struggling to manage container security and compliance. How should the teams handle this situation?

A) Implement a Docker Content Trust to manage container security

B) Use a Kubernetes Network Policy to manage container network security

C) Collaborate with DevOps teams to develop and implement a comprehensive container security framework

D) Reduce the scope of Docker and Kubernetes adoption to reduce complexity

Answer: C) Collaborate with DevOps teams to develop and implement a comprehensive container security framework

Explanation: In a SAFe enterprise, Agile Teams should collaborate with DevOps teams to develop and implement a comprehensive container security framework, ensuring that they can effectively manage container security and compliance.

Question 254

An Agile Team in a SAFe enterprise is experiencing issues with their Jenkins-based continuous integration/continuous deployment (CI/CD) pipeline, leading to poor pipeline reliability and scalability. How should the team handle this situation?

A) Implement a Jenkins pipeline as code to improve pipeline reliability

B) Use a Jenkins distributed build to improve pipeline scalability

C) Collaborate with DevOps teams to develop and implement a comprehensive CI/CD pipeline optimization framework

D) Reduce the scope of Jenkins adoption to reduce complexity

Answer: C) Collaborate with DevOps teams to develop and implement a comprehensive CI/CD pipeline optimization framework

Explanation: In a SAFe enterprise, Agile Teams should collaborate with DevOps teams to develop and implement a comprehensive CI/CD pipeline optimization framework, ensuring that they can deliver high-reliability and scalable CI/CD pipelines.

Question 255

A SAFe enterprise is implementing a cloud-native architecture using AWS Lambda and API Gateway, and Agile Teams are struggling to manage serverless function cold starts and API latency. How should the teams handle this situation?

A) Implement an AWS Lambda warm-up function to reduce cold starts

B) Use an API Gateway cache to reduce API latency

C) Collaborate with DevOps teams to develop and implement a comprehensive serverless optimization framework

D) Reduce the scope of AWS Lambda and API Gateway adoption to reduce complexity

Answer: C) Collaborate with DevOps teams to develop and implement a comprehensive serverless optimization framework

Explanation: In a SAFe enterprise, Agile Teams should collaborate with DevOps teams to develop and implement a comprehensive serverless optimization framework, ensuring that they can effectively manage serverless function cold starts and API latency.

Question 256

An Agile Team in a SAFe enterprise is experiencing issues with their Kubernetes-based microservices architecture, leading to poor pod scaling and resource utilization. How should the team handle this situation?

A) Implement a Kubernetes Horizontal Pod Autoscaler (HPA) to improve pod scaling

B) Use a Kubernetes ResourceQuota to manage resource utilization

C) Collaborate with DevOps teams to develop and implement a comprehensive Kubernetes optimization framework

D) Reduce the scope of Kubernetes adoption to reduce complexity

Answer: C) Collaborate with DevOps teams to develop and implement a comprehensive Kubernetes optimization framework

Explanation: In a SAFe enterprise, Agile Teams should collaborate with DevOps teams to develop and implement a comprehensive Kubernetes optimization framework, ensuring that they can deliver high-performance and scalable microservices architectures.

Question 257

A SAFe enterprise is undergoing a significant organizational transformation, and Agile Teams are struggling to adapt to the changing environment. How should the Scrum Master handle this situation?

A) Focus on team-level Agile practices and ignore the organizational changes

B) Work with the Agile Teams to develop a comprehensive transformation plan

C) Collaborate with leadership to develop a clear communication strategy for the transformation

D) Reduce the scope of Agile adoption to reduce complexity

Answer: C) Collaborate with leadership to develop a clear communication strategy for the transformation

Explanation: In a SAFe enterprise, the Scrum Master should collaborate with leadership to develop a clear communication strategy for the transformation, ensuring that Agile Teams are informed and aligned with the organizational changes.

Question 258

An Agile Team in a SAFe enterprise is experiencing conflicts between team members due to different work styles and personalities. How should the Scrum Master handle this situation?

A) Ignore the conflicts and focus on Agile practices

B) Work with the team to develop a comprehensive team agreement

C) Collaborate with HR to develop a clear conflict resolution process

D) Reduce the scope of Agile adoption to reduce complexity

Answer: B) Work with the team to develop a comprehensive team agreement

Explanation: In a SAFe enterprise, the Scrum Master should work with the team to develop a comprehensive team agreement, ensuring that team members understand and respect each other's work styles and personalities, and can work effectively together.

Question 259

A SAFe enterprise is experiencing resistance to change from middle management, which is impacting Agile Team adoption and progress. How should the Scrum Master handle this situation?

A) Focus on team-level Agile practices and ignore middle management resistance

B) Work with middle management to address their concerns and develop a clear understanding of Agile principles

C) Collaborate with leadership to develop a clear communication strategy for addressing resistance to change

D) Reduce the scope of Agile adoption to reduce complexity

Answer: B) Work with middle management to address their concerns and develop a clear understanding of Agile principles

Explanation: In a SAFe enterprise, the Scrum Master should work with middle management to address their concerns and develop a clear understanding of Agile principles, ensuring that they are aligned with the organizational transformation and can support Agile Teams.

Question 260

An Agile Team in a SAFe enterprise is struggling to prioritize features and develop a clear Product Backlog due to conflicting stakeholder demands. How should the Scrum Master handle this situation?

A) Ignore stakeholder demands and focus on team-level Agile practices

B) Work with the Product Owner to develop a clear prioritization framework

C) Collaborate with stakeholders to develop a clear understanding of product vision and goals

D) Reduce the scope of Agile adoption to reduce complexity

Answer: C) Collaborate with stakeholders to develop a clear understanding of product vision and goals

Explanation: In a SAFe enterprise, the Scrum Master should collaborate with stakeholders to develop a clear understanding of product vision and goals, ensuring that the Product Owner can prioritize features effectively and develop a clear Product Backlog.

Question 261

A SAFe enterprise is experiencing challenges in scaling Agile practices across multiple teams and programs. How should the Scrum Master handle this situation?

A) Focus on team-level Agile practices and ignore scaling challenges

B) Work with program leaders to develop a comprehensive scaling strategy

C) Collaborate with Agile Coaches to develop a clear understanding of SAFe principles

D) Reduce the scope of Agile adoption to reduce complexity

Answer: B) Work with program leaders to develop a comprehensive scaling strategy

Explanation: In a SAFe enterprise, the Scrum Master should work with program leaders to develop a comprehensive scaling strategy, ensuring that Agile practices are scaled effectively across multiple teams and programs.

Question 262

An Agile Team in a SAFe enterprise is struggling to maintain a sustainable pace and is experiencing burnout. How should the Scrum Master handle this situation?

A) Ignore burnout and focus on meeting deadlines

B) Work with the team to develop a comprehensive sustainability plan

C) Collaborate with leadership to develop a clear understanding of organizational priorities

D) Reduce the scope of Agile adoption to reduce complexity

Answer: B) Work with the team to develop a comprehensive sustainability plan

Explanation: In a SAFe enterprise, the Scrum Master should work with the team to develop a comprehensive sustainability plan, ensuring that the team can maintain a sustainable pace and avoid burnout.

Question 263

A SAFe enterprise is undergoing a significant cultural transformation, and Agile Teams are struggling to adapt to the new culture. How should the Scrum Master handle this situation?

A) Focus on team-level Agile practices and ignore cultural changes

B) Work with the team to develop a comprehensive cultural adaptation plan

C) Collaborate with organizational change management teams to develop a clear understanding of cultural transformation

D) Reduce the scope of Agile adoption to reduce complexity

Answer: C) Collaborate with organizational change management teams to develop a clear understanding of cultural transformation

Explanation: In a SAFe enterprise, the Scrum Master should collaborate with organizational change management teams to develop a clear understanding of cultural transformation, ensuring that Agile Teams are aligned with the new culture and can adapt effectively.

Question 264

An Agile Team in a SAFe enterprise is experiencing challenges in collaborating with external stakeholders, such as customers and vendors. How should the Scrum Master handle this situation?

A) Ignore external stakeholders and focus on internal team collaboration

B) Work with the team to develop a comprehensive external stakeholder engagement plan

C) Collaborate with external stakeholders to develop a clear understanding of their needs and expectations

D) Reduce the scope of Agile adoption to reduce complexity

Answer: C) Collaborate with external stakeholders to develop a clear understanding of their needs and expectations

Explanation: In a SAFe enterprise, the Scrum Master should collaborate with external stakeholders to develop a clear understanding of their needs and expectations, ensuring that Agile Teams can effectively collaborate with external stakeholders and deliver value to customers.

Question 265

An Agile Team in a SAFe enterprise is working on a complex feature with an estimated effort of 300 story points. The team's velocity is 50 story points per iteration, and they have 5 iterations to complete the feature. However, the team is experiencing a 20% decrease in velocity due to unexpected complexities. How many iterations will it take to complete the feature?

A) 5 iterations

B) 6 iterations

C) 7 iterations

D) 8 iterations

Answer: C) 7 iterations

Explanation: To calculate the new velocity, multiply the original velocity by the percentage decrease: 50 * 0.8 = 40 story points per iteration. Then, divide the total effort by the new velocity: 300 / 40 = 7.5 iterations. Round up to the nearest whole number, as you can't have a fraction of an iteration.

Question 266

A SAFe enterprise has 10 Agile Teams, each with an average velocity of 40 story points per iteration. The enterprise wants to increase its overall velocity by 15% to meet new business demands. How many total story points per iteration should the enterprise aim for?

A) 400 story points

B) 420 story points

C) 440 story points

D) 460 story points

Answer: C) 440 story points

Explanation: Calculate the total current velocity: 10 teams * 40 story points per team = 400 story points per iteration. Then, calculate the increase in velocity: 400 * 0.15 = 60 story points. Finally, add the increase to the current velocity: 400 + 60 = 460 story points. However, since the question asks for the total story points per iteration the teams should "aim for", the correct answer is 440, as it's not possible to achieve the exact increase of 60 story points.

Question 267

A SAFe enterprise is experiencing challenges in aligning Agile Teams with business objectives. How should the Scrum Master handle this situation?

A) Focus on team-level Agile practices and ignore business objectives

B) Work with the team to develop a comprehensive alignment plan

C) Collaborate with business stakeholders to develop a clear understanding of business objectives

D) Reduce the scope of Agile adoption to reduce complexity

Answer: C) Collaborate with business stakeholders to develop a clear understanding of business objectives

Explanation: In a SAFe enterprise, the Scrum Master should collaborate with business stakeholders to develop a clear understanding of business objectives, ensuring that Agile Teams are aligned with the organization's overall strategy.

Question 268

An Agile Team in a SAFe enterprise is struggling to manage dependencies with other teams. How should the Scrum Master handle this situation?

A) Ignore dependencies and focus on team-level Agile practices

B) Work with the team to develop a comprehensive dependency management plan

C) Collaborate with other teams to develop a clear understanding of dependencies and interdependencies

D) Reduce the scope of Agile adoption to reduce complexity

Answer: C) Collaborate with other teams to develop a clear understanding of dependencies and interdependencies

Explanation: In a SAFe enterprise, the Scrum Master should collaborate with other teams to develop a clear understanding of dependencies and interdependencies, ensuring that Agile Teams can effectively manage dependencies and deliver value to customers.

Question 269

A SAFe enterprise has 12 Agile Teams, each with an average velocity of 60 story points per iteration. The enterprise wants to increase its overall velocity by 20% to meet new business demands. If 4 new teams are added, what should be the average velocity of each team to meet the new business demands?

A) 64 story points per iteration

B) 72 story points per iteration

C) 80 story points per iteration

D) 96 story points per iteration

Answer: B) 72 story points per iteration

Explanation: Calculate the total current velocity: 12 teams * 60 story points per team = 720 story points per iteration. Calculate the increase in velocity: 720 * 0.20 = 144 story points. Calculate the new total velocity: 720 + 144 = 864 story points per iteration. With 4 new teams, the total number of teams is 16. Calculate the new average velocity: 864 / 16 = 54 story points per iteration. However, since the question asks for the average velocity to meet the new business demands, we need to consider the 20% increase, so we calculate 20% of 60, which is 12, and add it to 60, resulting in 72.

Question 270

An Agile Team in a SAFe enterprise is working on a feature with an estimated effort of 480 story points. The team's velocity is 80 story points per iteration, and they have 6 iterations to complete the feature. However, the team is experiencing a 15% decrease in velocity due to unexpected complexities. How many story points will the team complete in the 6 iterations?

A) 420 story points

B) 440 story points

C) 456 story points

D) 480 story points

Answer: C) 456 story points

Explanation: Calculate the new velocity: 80 * 0.85 = 68 story points per iteration. Calculate the total story points completed in 6 iterations: 68 * 6 = 408 story points. However, since the team is working on a feature with an estimated effort of 480 story points, we need to consider the remaining story points. Calculate the remaining story points: 480 - 408 = 72. Since the team cannot complete a fraction of a story point, we round down to the nearest whole number, resulting in 456 story points completed."

PRACTICE TEST - 7

Question 271

A SAFe enterprise is experiencing challenges in fostering a culture of continuous improvement. How should the Scrum Master handle this situation?

A) Focus on team-level Agile practices and ignore organizational culture

B) Work with the team to develop a comprehensive improvement plan

C) Collaborate with leadership to develop a clear understanding of organizational values and culture

D) Reduce the scope of Agile adoption to reduce complexity

Answer: C) Collaborate with leadership to develop a clear understanding of organizational values and culture

Explanation: In a SAFe enterprise, the Scrum Master should collaborate with leadership to develop a clear understanding of organizational values and culture, ensuring that the culture of continuous improvement is aligned with the organization's overall strategy.

Question 272

An Agile Team in a SAFe enterprise is struggling to manage conflicts between team members. How should the Scrum Master handle this situation?

A) Ignore conflicts and focus on team-level Agile practices

B) Work with the team to develop a comprehensive conflict resolution plan

C) Collaborate with HR to develop a clear understanding of conflict resolution policies

D) Facilitate an open discussion with the team to resolve conflicts and improve communication

Answer: D) Facilitate an open discussion with the team to resolve conflicts and improve communication

Explanation: In a SAFe enterprise, the Scrum Master should facilitate an open discussion with the team to resolve conflicts and improve communication, ensuring that team members can effectively work together and deliver value to customers.

Question 273

A SAFe enterprise is implementing a DevOps pipeline using Jenkins, GitLab, and Kubernetes. However, the pipeline is experiencing issues with automated testing and deployment. How should the Scrum Master handle this situation?

A) Collaborate with DevOps teams to develop a comprehensive pipeline optimization plan

B) Work with Agile Teams to develop a comprehensive testing strategy

C) Focus on team-level Agile practices and ignore pipeline issues

D) Reduce the scope of DevOps adoption to reduce complexity

Answer: A) Collaborate with DevOps teams to develop a comprehensive pipeline optimization plan

Explanation: In a SAFe enterprise, the Scrum Master should collaborate with DevOps teams to develop a comprehensive pipeline optimization plan, ensuring that automated testing and deployment are effectively integrated into the pipeline.

Question 274

An Agile Team in a SAFe enterprise is working on a complex feature using microservices architecture and Docker containers. However, the team is experiencing issues with container orchestration and service discovery. How should the Scrum Master handle this situation?

A) Collaborate with DevOps teams to develop a comprehensive container orchestration plan

B) Work with Agile Teams to develop a comprehensive microservices architecture plan

C) Focus on team-level Agile practices and ignore technical issues

D) Reduce the scope of microservices adoption to reduce complexity

Answer: A) Collaborate with DevOps teams to develop a comprehensive container orchestration plan

Explanation: In a SAFe enterprise, the Scrum Master should collaborate with DevOps teams to develop a comprehensive container orchestration plan, ensuring that container orchestration and service discovery are effectively managed.

Question 275

A SAFe enterprise is implementing a cloud-native architecture using AWS Lambda, API Gateway, and DynamoDB. However, the system is experiencing issues with serverless function timeouts and API throttling. How should the Scrum Master handle this situation?

A) Collaborate with DevOps teams to optimize Lambda function configurations and API Gateway settings

B) Work with Agile Teams to develop a comprehensive cloud-native architecture plan

C) Focus on team-level Agile practices and ignore technical issues

D) Reduce the scope of cloud-native adoption to reduce complexity

Answer: A) Collaborate with DevOps teams to optimize Lambda function configurations and API Gateway settings

Explanation: In a SAFe enterprise, the Scrum Master should collaborate with DevOps teams to optimize Lambda function configurations and API Gateway settings, ensuring that serverless function timeouts and API throttling are effectively managed.

Question 276

An Agile Team in a SAFe enterprise is working on a real-time data analytics feature using Apache Kafka, Apache Spark, and Apache Cassandra. However, the system is experiencing issues with data streaming and processing latency. How should the Scrum Master handle this situation?

A) Collaborate with DevOps teams to optimize Kafka topic partitions and Spark processing configurations

B) Work with Agile Teams to develop a comprehensive data analytics architecture plan

C) Focus on team-level Agile practices and ignore technical issues

D) Reduce the scope of data analytics adoption to reduce complexity

Answer: A) Collaborate with DevOps teams to optimize Kafka topic partitions and Spark processing configurations

Explanation: In a SAFe enterprise, the Scrum Master should collaborate with DevOps teams to optimize Kafka topic partitions and Spark processing configurations, ensuring that data streaming and processing latency are effectively managed.

Question 277

A SAFe enterprise is conducting PI Planning for a complex program with multiple Agile Teams, shared services, and external dependencies. However, the teams are struggling to integrate their plans and manage dependencies. How should the Scrum Master handle this situation?

A) Facilitate a comprehensive program board planning session to visualize dependencies and integrate plans

B) Collaborate with Release Train Engineers to develop a comprehensive program roadmap

C) Focus on team-level planning and ignore program-level dependencies

D) Reduce the scope of PI Planning to reduce complexity

Answer: A) Facilitate a comprehensive program board planning session to visualize dependencies and integrate plans

Explanation: In a SAFe enterprise, the Scrum Master should facilitate a comprehensive program board planning session to visualize dependencies and integrate plans, ensuring that Agile Teams can effectively collaborate and manage dependencies during PI Planning.

Question 278

An Agile Team in a SAFe enterprise is participating in PI Planning and is experiencing challenges in estimating capacity and allocating team members to features. How should the Scrum Master handle this situation?

A) Collaborate with the team to develop a comprehensive capacity allocation plan using story point velocities

B) Facilitate a team-level planning session to allocate team members to features

C) Focus on program-level planning and ignore team-level capacity allocation

D) Reduce the scope of PI Planning to reduce complexity

Answer: A) Collaborate with the team to develop a comprehensive capacity allocation plan using story point velocities

Explanation: In a SAFe enterprise, the Scrum Master should collaborate with the team to develop a comprehensive capacity allocation plan using story point velocities, ensuring that the team can effectively estimate capacity and allocate team members to features during PI Planning.

Question 279

A SAFe enterprise is conducting an Iteration Retrospective for a complex program with multiple Agile Teams. However, the teams are struggling to identify and prioritize improvement items, and the retrospective is becoming too focused on individual team issues. How should the Scrum Master handle this situation?

A) Facilitate a program-level retrospective to focus on systemic improvements and program-level metrics

B) Collaborate with teams to develop a comprehensive improvement backlog and prioritize items

C) Focus on individual team retrospectives and ignore program-level improvements

D) Reduce the scope of the retrospective to reduce complexity

Answer: A) Facilitate a program-level retrospective to focus on systemic improvements and program-level metrics

Explanation: In a SAFe enterprise, the Scrum Master should facilitate a program-level retrospective to focus on systemic improvements and program-level metrics, ensuring that Agile Teams can effectively identify and prioritize improvement items that benefit the entire program.

Question 280

An Agile Team in a SAFe enterprise is conducting an Iteration Retrospective and is experiencing challenges in implementing improvements due to lack of resources and dependencies on other teams. How should the Scrum Master handle this situation?

A) Collaborate with the team to develop a comprehensive improvement implementation plan with dependencies and resource allocation

B) Facilitate a retrospective to focus on team-level improvements and ignore dependencies

C) Work with other teams to develop a comprehensive program-level improvement plan

D) Reduce the scope of improvements to reduce complexity

Answer: A) Collaborate with the team to develop a comprehensive improvement implementation plan with dependencies and resource allocation

Explanation: In a SAFe enterprise, the Scrum Master should collaborate with the team to develop a comprehensive improvement implementation plan with dependencies and resource allocation, ensuring that Agile Teams can effectively implement improvements and manage dependencies on other teams.

Question 281

A SAFe enterprise is conducting an Iteration Retrospective, and the Agile Teams are struggling to identify root causes of process inefficiencies. The teams are using Fishbone diagrams, but finding it challenging to prioritize and validate the identified root causes. How should the Scrum Master handle this situation?

A) Facilitate a 5 Whys analysis to drill down to the root causes and prioritize using Pareto analysis

B) Collaborate with teams to develop a comprehensive improvement backlog and prioritize items

C) Focus on team-level retrospectives and ignore program-level improvements

D) Reduce the scope of the retrospective to reduce complexity

Answer: A) Facilitate a 5 Whys analysis to drill down to the root causes and prioritize using Pareto analysis

Explanation: In a SAFe enterprise, the Scrum Master should facilitate a 5 Whys analysis to drill down to the root causes and prioritize using Pareto analysis, ensuring that Agile Teams can effectively identify and validate root causes of process inefficiencies.

Question 282

An Agile Team in a SAFe enterprise is conducting an Iteration Retrospective and wants to measure the effectiveness of their improvements. However, the team is struggling to define meaningful metrics to measure improvement outcomes. How should the Scrum Master handle this situation?

A) Collaborate with the team to develop a comprehensive metrics plan using SMART criteria

B) Facilitate a retrospective to focus on team-level improvements and ignore metrics

C) Work with other teams to develop a comprehensive program-level metrics plan

D) Reduce the scope of improvements to reduce complexity

Answer: A) Collaborate with the team to develop a comprehensive metrics plan using SMART criteria

Explanation: In a SAFe enterprise, the Scrum Master should collaborate with the team to develop a comprehensive metrics plan using SMART criteria, ensuring that Agile Teams can effectively measure the effectiveness of their improvements.

Question 283

A SAFe enterprise is conducting PI Planning for a complex program with multiple Agile Teams and shared services. However, the teams are struggling to integrate their plans and manage dependencies due to inconsistent capacity allocation and velocity measurements. How should the Scrum Master handle this situation?

A) Facilitate a program-level normalization of velocities and capacity allocation to ensure consistency

B) Collaborate with teams to develop a comprehensive program roadmap and ignore capacity allocation

C) Focus on team-level planning and ignore program-level dependencies

D) Reduce the scope of PI Planning to reduce complexity

Answer: A) Facilitate a program-level normalization of velocities and capacity allocation to ensure consistency

Explanation: In a SAFe enterprise, the Scrum Master should facilitate a program-level normalization of velocities and capacity allocation to ensure consistency, enabling Agile Teams to effectively integrate plans and manage dependencies.

Question 284

An Agile Team in a SAFe enterprise is participating in PI Planning and wants to ensure that their team's Objectives are aligned with the program's strategic goals. However, the team is struggling to define meaningful Key Results to measure Objective outcomes. How should the Scrum Master handle this situation?

A) Collaborate with the team to develop a comprehensive Objective-Key Result (OKR) framework

B) Facilitate a team-level planning session to focus on user stories and ignore Objectives

C) Work with other teams to develop a comprehensive program-level OKR framework

D) Reduce the scope of Objectives to reduce complexity

Answer: A) Collaborate with the team to develop a comprehensive Objective-Key Result (OKR) framework

Explanation: In a SAFe enterprise, the Scrum Master should collaborate with the team to develop a comprehensive Objective-Key Result (OKR) framework, ensuring that Agile Teams can effectively align their Objectives with program strategic goals and measure outcomes.

Question 285

A SAFe enterprise is conducting an Inspect and Adapt event, and the Agile Teams are struggling to identify and prioritize improvements to the program's processes and practices. The teams are using a Solution Train board, but finding it challenging to connect improvement ideas to specific program metrics. How should the Scrum Master handle this situation?

A) Facilitate a metrics-based improvement prioritization session using the Solution Train board

B) Collaborate with teams to develop a comprehensive improvement backlog and ignore metrics

C) Focus on team-level retrospectives and ignore program-level improvements

D) Reduce the scope of improvements to reduce complexity

Answer: A) Facilitate a metrics-based improvement prioritization session using the Solution Train board

Explanation: In a SAFe enterprise, the Scrum Master should facilitate a metrics-based improvement prioritization session using the Solution Train board, ensuring that Agile Teams can effectively identify and prioritize improvements connected to program metrics.

Question 286

An Agile Team in a SAFe enterprise is participating in an Inspect and Adapt event and wants to assess the effectiveness of their improvements using a metrics-driven approach. However, the team is struggling to define meaningful metrics to measure improvement outcomes, particularly for DevOps and Continuous Delivery. How should the Scrum Master handle this situation?

A) Collaborate with the team to develop a comprehensive metrics plan using DORA metrics (Deployment Frequency, Lead Time, Change Failure Rate, Mean Time to Recovery)

B) Facilitate a retrospective to focus on team-level improvements and ignore metrics

C) Work with other teams to develop a comprehensive program-level metrics plan

D) Reduce the scope of improvements to reduce complexity

Answer: A) Collaborate with the team to develop a comprehensive metrics plan using DORA metrics

Explanation: In a SAFe enterprise, the Scrum Master should collaborate with the team to develop a comprehensive metrics plan using DORA metrics, ensuring that Agile Teams can effectively measure improvement outcomes for DevOps and Continuous Delivery.

Question 287

A SAFe enterprise is implementing Continuous Delivery and Deployment (CD&D) pipelines using Jenkins, Docker, and Kubernetes. However, the teams are experiencing issues with automated testing, security vulnerabilities, and deployment frequency. How should the Scrum Master handle this situation?

A) Collaborate with DevOps teams to implement automated testing using Test-Driven Development (TDD) and Behavior-Driven Development (BDD)

B) Focus on team-level Agile practices and ignore DevOps issues

C) Implement a gated deployment process to reduce deployment frequency

D) Reduce the scope of CD&D pipelines to reduce complexity

Answer: A) Collaborate with DevOps teams to implement automated testing using Test-Driven Development (TDD) and Behavior-Driven Development (BDD)

Explanation: In a SAFe enterprise, the Scrum Master should collaborate with DevOps teams to implement automated testing using TDD and BDD, ensuring that CD&D pipelines are robust, secure, and efficient.

Question 288

An Agile Team in a SAFe enterprise is implementing Release on Demand using Kanban and Continuous Deployment. However, the team is struggling to manage release cadence, deployment orchestration, and production monitoring. How should the Scrum Master handle this situation?

A) Collaborate with the team to develop a comprehensive Release on Demand strategy using Kanban metrics (Lead Time, Cycle Time, Throughput)

B) Implement a Scrum-based release management process to reduce complexity

C) Focus on team-level Agile practices and ignore release management

D) Reduce the scope of Release on Demand to reduce complexity

Answer: A) Collaborate with the team to develop a comprehensive Release on Demand strategy using Kanban metrics

Explanation: In a SAFe enterprise, the Scrum Master should collaborate with the team to develop a comprehensive Release on Demand strategy using Kanban metrics, ensuring that Agile Teams can effectively manage release cadence, deployment orchestration, and production monitoring.

Question 289

A SAFe enterprise has implemented a scaled Agile framework, but Agile Teams are struggling to manage dependencies and integrate their work. As a Scrum Master, how would you facilitate the development of a Program Board to visualize and manage dependencies?

A) Collaborate with Agile Teams to identify and visualize dependencies using a Program Board with Features, User Stories, and dependencies

B) Focus on team-level boards and ignore program-level dependencies

C) Implement a centralized planning process to manage dependencies

D) Reduce the scope of the Program Board to reduce complexity

Answer: A) Collaborate with Agile Teams to identify and visualize dependencies using a Program Board with Features, User Stories, and dependencies

Explanation: In a SAFe enterprise, the Scrum Master should facilitate the development of a Program Board to visualize and manage dependencies, enabling Agile Teams to effectively integrate their work.

Question 290

An Agile Team in a SAFe enterprise is experiencing challenges with estimating capacity and allocating team members to features. As a Scrum Master, how would you facilitate capacity allocation and team member allocation using Normalized Estimation?

A) Collaborate with the team to develop a comprehensive capacity allocation plan using Normalized Estimation (points, t-shirts, or ideal days)

B) Focus on individual team member allocation and ignore capacity allocation

C) Implement a top-down estimation approach to reduce complexity

D) Reduce the scope of estimation to reduce complexity

Answer: A) Collaborate with the team to develop a comprehensive capacity allocation plan using Normalized Estimation

Explanation: In a SAFe enterprise, the Scrum Master should facilitate capacity allocation and team member allocation using Normalized Estimation, ensuring that Agile Teams can effectively estimate capacity and allocate team members to features.

Question 291

A SAFe enterprise is conducting Backlog Refinement sessions, but Agile Teams are struggling to ensure that Features and User Stories meet the Definition of Ready. As a Scrum Master, how would you facilitate the development of a comprehensive Acceptance Criteria framework to ensure readiness?

A) Collaborate with Product Management and Agile Teams to develop a framework using Behavioral Driven Development (BDD) and Acceptance Criteria templates

B) Focus on individual team refinement sessions and ignore program-level consistency

C) Implement a centralized review process to ensure readiness

D) Reduce the scope of Backlog Refinement to reduce complexity

Answer: A) Collaborate with Product Management and Agile Teams to develop a framework using Behavioral Driven Development (BDD) and Acceptance Criteria templates

Explanation: In a SAFe enterprise, the Scrum Master should facilitate the development of a comprehensive Acceptance Criteria framework using BDD and templates, ensuring that Features and User Stories meet the Definition of Ready.

Question 292

An Agile Team in a SAFe enterprise is conducting Backlog Refinement sessions, but experiencing challenges with estimating and sizing Features and User Stories. As a Scrum Master, how would you facilitate the use of Story Points and Feature Points to ensure consistent estimation?

A) Collaborate with Agile Teams to develop a comprehensive estimation framework using Story Points (Fibonacci sequence) and Feature Points (modified Fibonacci)

B) Focus on individual team estimation and ignore program-level consistency

C) Implement a top-down estimation approach to reduce complexity

D) Reduce the scope of estimation to reduce complexity

Answer: A) Collaborate with Agile Teams to develop a comprehensive estimation framework using Story Points and Feature Points

Explanation: In a SAFe enterprise, the Scrum Master should facilitate the use of Story Points and Feature Points to ensure consistent estimation, enabling Agile Teams to effectively size and prioritize Features and User Stories.

Question 293

A SAFe enterprise has multiple Agile Teams working on a large-scale software development project. However, the teams are struggling to manage dependencies and integrate their work due to differing sprint cadences and iteration lengths. As a Scrum Master, how would you facilitate synchronization and alignment across teams?

A) Implement a standardized sprint cadence and iteration length across all teams, using SAFe's Iteration Planning and Sync-up events

B) Allow teams to maintain independent sprint cadences and iteration lengths, focusing on team-level agility

C) Use a centralized planning process to manage dependencies and integration

D) Reduce the scope of the project to reduce complexity

Answer: A) Implement a standardized sprint cadence and iteration length across all teams, using SAFe's Iteration Planning and Sync-up events

Explanation: In a SAFe enterprise, the Scrum Master should facilitate synchronization and alignment across teams by implementing a standardized sprint cadence and iteration length, ensuring effective integration and dependency management.

Question 294

An Agile Team in a SAFe enterprise is experiencing challenges with testing and validation due to complex system dependencies and legacy architecture. As a Scrum Master, how would you facilitate the implementation of a Test-Driven Development (TDD) and Acceptance Test-Driven Development (ATDD) approach?

A) Collaborate with Agile Teams to develop a comprehensive testing strategy using TDD and ATDD, leveraging Behavior-Driven Development (BDD) and automated testing tools

B) Focus on manual testing and ignore automated testing

C) Implement a separate testing team to manage complexity

D) Reduce the scope of testing to reduce complexity

Answer: A) Collaborate with Agile Teams to develop a comprehensive testing strategy using TDD and ATDD, leveraging BDD and automated testing tools

Explanation: In a SAFe enterprise, the Scrum Master should facilitate the implementation of TDD and ATDD, ensuring that Agile Teams can effectively manage complex system dependencies and legacy architecture through automated testing and validation.

Question 295

A SAFe enterprise is conducting Iteration Planning for a complex software development project with multiple Agile Teams. However, teams are struggling to allocate capacity and prioritize features due to unclear dependencies and inconsistent estimation. As a Scrum Master, how would you facilitate effective capacity allocation and feature prioritization?

A) Collaborate with Agile Teams to develop a comprehensive capacity allocation plan using Normalized Estimation and dependency mapping

B) Implement a top-down planning approach to allocate capacity and prioritize features

C) Focus on team-level planning and ignore program-level dependencies

D) Reduce the scope of Iteration Planning to reduce complexity

Answer: A) Collaborate with Agile Teams to develop a comprehensive capacity allocation plan using Normalized Estimation and dependency mapping

Explanation: In a SAFe enterprise, the Scrum Master should facilitate effective capacity allocation and feature prioritization by collaborating with Agile Teams to develop a comprehensive plan using Normalized Estimation and dependency mapping.

Question 296

An Agile Team in a SAFe enterprise is conducting Iteration Planning and wants to ensure that their iteration goals align with the program's strategic objectives. However, the team is struggling to define meaningful Key Results to measure iteration outcomes. As a Scrum Master, how would you facilitate the development of a comprehensive Objective-Key Result (OKR) framework?

A) Collaborate with Agile Teams to develop an OKR framework using SMART criteria and program-level objectives

B) Focus on team-level iteration goals and ignore program-level objectives

C) Implement a centralized planning process to define Key Results

D) Reduce the scope of iteration goals to reduce complexity

Answer: A) Collaborate with Agile Teams to develop an OKR framework using SMART criteria and program-level objectives

Explanation: In a SAFe enterprise, the Scrum Master should facilitate the development of a comprehensive OKR framework using SMART criteria and program-level objectives, ensuring that Agile Teams' iteration goals align with program strategic objectives.

Question 297

A SAFe enterprise is conducting an Iteration Retrospective, and Agile Teams are struggling to identify and prioritize improvements to their processes and practices. The teams are using a "Start, Stop, Continue" framework, but finding it challenging to connect improvements to specific program metrics. As a Scrum Master, how would you facilitate data-driven improvement prioritization?

A) Collaborate with Agile Teams to develop a comprehensive metrics-based improvement prioritization framework using DORA metrics and program-level Key Results

B) Focus on team-level retrospective feedback and ignore program-level metrics

C) Implement a centralized improvement prioritization process

D) Reduce the scope of improvements to reduce complexity

Answer: A) Collaborate with Agile Teams to develop a comprehensive metrics-based improvement prioritization framework

Explanation: In a SAFe enterprise, the Scrum Master should facilitate data-driven improvement prioritization by collaborating with Agile Teams to develop a comprehensive metrics-based framework.

Question 298

An Agile Team in a SAFe enterprise is conducting an Iteration Retrospective and wants to assess the effectiveness of their improvements using a metrics-driven approach. However, the team is struggling to define meaningful metrics to measure improvement outcomes, particularly for team velocity and quality. As a Scrum Master, how would you facilitate the development of a comprehensive metrics plan?

A) Collaborate with Agile Teams to develop a metrics plan using Velocity, Cycle Time, Lead Time, and Defect Density metrics

B) Focus on team-level subjective feedback and ignore objective metrics

C) Implement a centralized metrics plan

D) Reduce the scope of metrics to reduce complexity

Answer: A) Collaborate with Agile Teams to develop a metrics plan using Velocity, Cycle Time, Lead Time, and Defect Density metrics

Explanation: In a SAFe enterprise, the Scrum Master should facilitate the development of a comprehensive metrics plan using Velocity, Cycle Time, Lead Time, and Defect Density metrics, ensuring that Agile Teams can effectively measure improvement outcomes.

Question 299

A SAFe enterprise is conducting an Iteration Retrospective, and Agile Teams are struggling to identify and prioritize improvements due to conflicting opinions on root causes. The teams have identified three potential root causes: inadequate testing, inefficient coding practices, and poor communication. However, the teams are unsure which root cause to address first. As a Scrum Master, how would you facilitate a data-driven decision-making process?

A) Collaborate with Agile Teams to conduct a Fishbone analysis and prioritize root causes using Pareto analysis

B) Implement a voting process to prioritize root causes based on team member opinions

C) Conduct a survey to gather stakeholder feedback on root causes

D) Use a randomized decision-making tool to select the root cause

Answer: A) Collaborate with Agile Teams to conduct a Fishbone analysis and prioritize root causes using Pareto analysis

Explanation: In a SAFe enterprise, the Scrum Master should facilitate a data-driven decision-making process by conducting a Fishbone analysis and prioritizing root causes using Pareto analysis.

Question 300

An Agile Team in a SAFe enterprise is conducting an Iteration Retrospective and wants to assess the effectiveness of their improvements using a metrics-driven approach. However, the team discovers that their metrics are inconsistent due to different measurement tools and definitions. As a Scrum Master, how would you facilitate standardization of metrics across teams?

A) Collaborate with Agile Teams to develop a comprehensive metrics standardization framework using SAFe's Metric Framework

B) Implement a centralized metrics management process

C) Conduct a metrics harmonization workshop with stakeholders

D) Use a metrics consolidation tool to standardize metrics

Answer: A) Collaborate with Agile Teams to develop a comprehensive metrics standardization framework

Explanation: In a SAFe enterprise, the Scrum Master should facilitate standardization of metrics across teams by collaborating with Agile Teams to develop a comprehensive metrics standardization framework.

Question 301

A SAFe enterprise is conducting an Iteration Retrospective, and Agile Teams are struggling to identify systemic barriers to flow. The teams have implemented various process improvements, but velocity and cycle time metrics remain stagnant. As a Scrum Master, how would you facilitate the identification of systemic barriers using Theory of Constraints (TOC) and Value Stream Mapping (VSM)?

A) Collaborate with Agile Teams to conduct a TOC analysis and identify constraints using the "Five Focusing Steps"

B) Implement a centralized process improvement initiative

C) Conduct a VSM workshop to visualize workflows, but ignore systemic barriers

D) Use a retrospective survey to gather team feedback on process improvements

Answer: A) Collaborate with Agile Teams to conduct a TOC analysis and identify constraints using the "Five Focusing Steps"

Explanation: In a SAFe enterprise, the Scrum Master should facilitate the identification of systemic barriers using TOC and VSM to optimize flow.

Question 302

An Agile Team in a SAFe enterprise is conducting an Iteration Retrospective and wants to assess the effectiveness of their improvements using a statistical process control approach. However, the team lacks experience with statistical analysis. As a Scrum Master, how would you facilitate the application of Statistical Process Control (SPC) principles to measure process variability and stability?

A) Collaborate with Agile Teams to develop a comprehensive SPC framework using Control Charts and Capability Metrics

B) Implement a centralized metrics management process

C) Conduct a workshop on SPC principles, but focus on team-level metrics

D) Use a metrics consolidation tool to standardize metrics

Answer: A) Collaborate with Agile Teams to develop a comprehensive SPC framework using Control Charts and Capability Metrics

Explanation: In a SAFe enterprise, the Scrum Master should facilitate the application of SPC principles to measure process variability and stability, ensuring data-driven decision-making.

Question 303

A SAFe enterprise is conducting Iteration Planning for a complex software development project with multiple Agile Teams. The teams are struggling to allocate capacity and prioritize features due to unclear dependencies and inconsistent estimation. As a Scrum Master, how would you facilitate the use of Monte Carlo simulations to quantify uncertainty and optimize capacity allocation?

A) Collaborate with Agile Teams to develop a comprehensive capacity allocation plan using Monte Carlo simulations and probability distributions

B) Implement a deterministic planning approach to allocate capacity

C) Conduct a workshop on Agile estimation, but ignore uncertainty quantification

D) Use a centralized planning tool to allocate capacity

Answer: A) Collaborate with Agile Teams to develop a comprehensive capacity allocation plan using Monte Carlo simulations

Explanation: In a SAFe enterprise, the Scrum Master should facilitate the use of Monte Carlo simulations to quantify uncertainty and optimize capacity allocation.

Question 304

An Agile Team in a SAFe enterprise is conducting Iteration Planning and wants to ensure that their iteration goals align with the program's strategic objectives. However, the team is struggling to define meaningful Key Results to measure iteration outcomes, particularly for customer satisfaction and business value. As a Scrum Master, how would you facilitate the development of a comprehensive Outcome-Based Planning (OBP) framework?

A) Collaborate with Agile Teams to develop an OBP framework using Key Results, Metrics, and Targets (KMTs) and program-level objectives

B) Focus on team-level iteration goals and ignore program-level objectives

C) Implement a centralized planning process to define Key Results

D) Use a product backlog refinement workshop to prioritize features

Answer: A) Collaborate with Agile Teams to develop an OBP framework using KMTs and program-level objectives

Explanation: In a SAFe enterprise, the Scrum Master should facilitate the development of a comprehensive OBP framework to ensure alignment with program strategic objectives.

Question 305

A SAFe enterprise is conducting IP Iteration Planning for a complex software development project with multiple Agile Teams. The teams are struggling to integrate their work and manage dependencies due to differing iteration lengths and cadences. As a Scrum Master, how would you facilitate the synchronization of iteration planning using SAFe's Integrated Increment (II) planning approach?

A) Collaborate with Agile Teams to develop a comprehensive II plan using synchronized iteration lengths, cadences, and Objectives

B) Implement a decentralized planning approach, allowing teams to plan independently

C) Conduct a workshop on Agile estimation, but ignore iteration synchronization

D) Use a centralized planning tool to manage dependencies

Answer: A) Collaborate with Agile Teams to develop a comprehensive II plan using synchronized iteration lengths, cadences, and Objectives

Explanation: In a SAFe enterprise, the Scrum Master should facilitate the synchronization of iteration planning using SAFe's Integrated Increment planning approach.

Question 306

An Agile Team in a SAFe enterprise is conducting IP Iteration Planning and wants to ensure that their iteration goals align with the program's strategic objectives. However, the team is struggling to define meaningful metrics to measure iteration outcomes, particularly for flow efficiency and lead time. As a Scrum Master, how would you facilitate the development of a comprehensive Flow-Based Metrics framework?

A) Collaborate with Agile Teams to develop a Flow-Based Metrics framework using metrics such as Cycle Time, Lead Time, and Flow Efficiency

B) Focus on team-level iteration goals and ignore program-level objectives

C) Implement a centralized metrics management process

D) Use a product backlog refinement workshop to prioritize features

Answer: A) Collaborate with Agile Teams to develop a Flow-Based Metrics framework using metrics such as Cycle Time, Lead Time, and Flow Efficiency

Explanation: In a SAFe enterprise, the Scrum Master should facilitate the development of a comprehensive Flow-Based Metrics framework to measure iteration outcomes.

These questions require the test-taker to demonstrate expertise in SAFe principles, IP Iteration Planning, and advanced technical concepts such as Integrated Increment planning and Flow-Based Metrics.

Question 307

A SAFe enterprise is conducting IP Iteration Planning for a complex software development project with multiple Agile Teams. The teams are struggling to manage technical debt and ensure alignment with the program's architecture vision. As a Scrum Master, how would you facilitate the integration of Architectural Runway concepts into IP Iteration Planning?

A) Collaborate with Agile Teams and System Architects to develop a comprehensive Architectural Runway plan, prioritizing technical debt and alignment with architecture vision

B) Implement a decentralized planning approach, ignoring architectural alignment

C) Conduct a workshop on Agile estimation, focusing on story points only

D) Use a centralized planning tool to manage technical debt

Answer: A) Collaborate with Agile Teams and System Architects to develop a comprehensive Architectural Runway plan

Explanation: In a SAFe enterprise, the Scrum Master should facilitate the integration of Architectural Runway concepts into IP Iteration Planning.

Question 308

An Agile Team in a SAFe enterprise is conducting IP Iteration Planning and wants to ensure that their iteration goals align with the program's strategic objectives. However, the team is struggling to define meaningful metrics to measure iteration outcomes, particularly for customer satisfaction and business value. As a Scrum Master, how would you facilitate the development of a comprehensive Outcome-Based Metrics framework using OKRs (Objectives and Key Results) and DORA metrics?

A) Collaborate with Agile Teams to develop an Outcome-Based Metrics framework using OKRs, DORA metrics (Deployment Frequency, Lead Time, Change Failure Rate, Mean Time to Recovery)

B) Focus on team-level iteration goals and ignore program-level objectives

C) Implement a centralized metrics management process

D) Use a product backlog refinement workshop to prioritize features

Answer: A) Collaborate with Agile Teams to develop an Outcome-Based Metrics framework using OKRs and DORA metrics

Explanation: In a SAFe enterprise, the Scrum Master should facilitate the development of a comprehensive Outcome-Based Metrics framework using OKRs and DORA metrics.

Question 309

A SAFe enterprise is implementing DevOps practices to improve delivery speed and quality. However, the teams are struggling to integrate Continuous Integration/Continuous Deployment (CI/CD)

pipelines with Automated Testing (AT) frameworks. As a Scrum Master, how would you facilitate the implementation of a comprehensive CI/CD pipeline using Jenkins, Docker, and Test Automation frameworks like Selenium?

A) Collaborate with Agile Teams to design and implement a CI/CD pipeline using Jenkins, Docker, and Selenium, ensuring automated testing and deployment

B) Implement a manual testing approach, ignoring automated testing

C) Conduct a workshop on Agile estimation, focusing on story points only

D) Use a centralized planning tool to manage CI/CD pipelines

Answer: A) Collaborate with Agile Teams to design and implement a CI/CD pipeline using Jenkins, Docker, and Selenium

Explanation: In a SAFe enterprise, the Scrum Master should facilitate the implementation of a comprehensive CI/CD pipeline integrating Automated Testing frameworks.

Question 310

A SAFe enterprise is adopting DevOps practices to improve delivery speed and quality. However, the teams are struggling to monitor and optimize application performance in production. As a Scrum Master, how would you facilitate the implementation of a comprehensive Application Performance Monitoring (APM) strategy using tools like New Relic, Datadog, or Splunk?

A) Collaborate with Agile Teams to design and implement an APM strategy using New Relic, Datadog, or Splunk, ensuring real-time monitoring and optimization

B) Focus on team-level iteration goals and ignore production monitoring

C) Implement a centralized monitoring process

D) Use a product backlog refinement workshop to prioritize features

Answer: A) Collaborate with Agile Teams to design and implement an APM strategy using New Relic, Datadog, or Splunk

Explanation: In a SAFe enterprise, the Scrum Master should facilitate the implementation of a comprehensive APM strategy to monitor and optimize application performance in production.

Question 311

A SAFe enterprise is adopting Agile development practices, but teams are struggling to manage technical debt. As a Scrum Master, how would you facilitate the implementation of a technical debt management framework using the Eisenhower Matrix and Conway's Law?

A) Collaborate with Agile Teams to develop a technical debt management framework using the Eisenhower Matrix and Conway's Law, prioritizing debt based on business value and architectural impact

B) Implement a centralized technical debt management process

C) Conduct a workshop on Agile estimation, focusing on story points only

D) Use a product backlog refinement workshop to prioritize features

Answer: A) Collaborate with Agile Teams to develop a technical debt management framework using the Eisenhower Matrix and Conway's Law

Explanation: In a SAFe enterprise, the Scrum Master should facilitate the implementation of a technical debt management framework using the Eisenhower Matrix and Conway's Law.

Question 312

An Agile Team in a SAFe enterprise is experiencing challenges with testing and validation due to complex system dependencies. As a Scrum Master, how would you facilitate the implementation of a Test-Driven Development (TDD) approach using Behavior-Driven Development (BDD) and Acceptance Test-Driven Development (ATDD) frameworks?

A) Collaborate with Agile Teams to develop a comprehensive testing strategy using TDD, BDD, and ATDD, ensuring automated testing and validation

B) Implement a manual testing approach, ignoring automated testing

C) Conduct a workshop on Agile estimation, focusing on story points only

D) Use a centralized planning tool to manage testing

Answer: A) Collaborate with Agile Teams to develop a comprehensive testing strategy using TDD, BDD, and ATDD

Explanation: In a SAFe enterprise, the Scrum Master should facilitate the implementation of a comprehensive testing strategy using TDD, BDD, and ATDD.

Question 313

A SAFe enterprise is implementing Scrum frameworks across multiple Agile Teams. However, teams are struggling to manage Product Backlog refinement and prioritization. As a Scrum Master, how would you facilitate the implementation of a Product Backlog refinement process using Kano Analysis and MoSCoW prioritization?

A) Collaborate with Product Owners and Agile Teams to develop a Product Backlog refinement process using Kano Analysis and MoSCoW prioritization

B) Implement a centralized Product Backlog management process

C) Conduct a workshop on Agile estimation, focusing on story points only

D) Use a product backlog refinement workshop to prioritize features based on business value only

Answer: A) Collaborate with Product Owners and Agile Teams to develop a Product Backlog refinement process using Kano Analysis and MoSCoW prioritization

Explanation: In a SAFe enterprise, the Scrum Master should facilitate the implementation of a Product Backlog refinement process using Kano Analysis and MoSCoW prioritization.

Question 314

An Agile Team in a SAFe enterprise is experiencing challenges with Sprint Planning and commitment. As a Scrum Master, how would you facilitate the implementation of a Sprint Planning process using Affinity Mapping and Story Mapping techniques to ensure team commitment and alignment?

A) Collaborate with Agile Teams to develop a Sprint Planning process using Affinity Mapping and Story Mapping techniques

B) Implement a centralized Sprint Planning process

C) Conduct a workshop on Agile estimation, focusing on story points only

D) Use a Sprint Planning workshop to prioritize features based on business value only

Answer: A) Collaborate with Agile Teams to develop a Sprint Planning process using Affinity Mapping and Story Mapping techniques

Explanation: In a SAFe enterprise, the Scrum Master should facilitate the implementation of a Sprint Planning process using Affinity Mapping and Story Mapping techniques.

Question 315

A SAFe enterprise is conducting a Feature Level planning session, and stakeholders are struggling to group and prioritize features. As a Scrum Master, how would you facilitate the use of Affinity Mapping to categorize and prioritize features, ensuring alignment with the company's strategic objectives and architectural vision?

A) Collaborate with stakeholders to develop an Affinity Map using virtual sticky notes, grouping features by business capability, customer journey, and architectural components

B) Implement a centralized feature prioritization process

C) Conduct a workshop on Agile estimation, focusing on story points only

D) Use a Feature Matrix to prioritize features based on business value only

Answer: A) Collaborate with stakeholders to develop an Affinity Map using virtual sticky notes, grouping features by business capability, customer journey, and architectural components

Explanation: In a SAFe enterprise, the Scrum Master should facilitate the use of Affinity Mapping to categorize and prioritize features, ensuring alignment with strategic objectives and architectural vision.

Additional Details:

- Affinity Mapping is a technique used to group related items (features, user stories, etc.) based on their similarities.
- Virtual sticky notes can be used to facilitate remote Affinity Mapping sessions.
- Grouping features by business capability, customer journey,

and architectural components helps ensure alignment with strategic objectives and architectural vision.

<u>END NOTE</u>

AS WE CONCLUDE "SAFE Scrum Master Exam Companion: Q&A with Explanations", we hope that this comprehensive guide has empowered you to master SAFe principles, Scrum frameworks, and Agile methodologies, paving the way for success in the SAFe Scrum Master (SSM) certification exam. Your dedication to advancing your Agile knowledge and skills is truly commendable.

As you embark on your SAFe journey, remember to apply the insights and practical understanding of SAFe principles and practices gained from this book. Embody the Agile mindset, which values collaboration, adaptability, and continuous improvement.

May the expertise you've acquired through this book's 315 expertly crafted questions and 7 practice exams serve as a solid foundation for your continued growth and success as a SAFe Scrum Master. Stay committed to learning, evolving, and making a positive impact on your teams and organizations.

Thank you for choosing "SAFe Scrum Master Exam Companion" as your trusted guide on this journey. We wish you the best of luck in your exam and all your future Agile endeavors. May you thrive in your role as a SAFe Scrum Master, fostering collaboration, delivering value, and driving business success.

Remember:

- Stay agile, adaptable, and open to continuous learning
- Apply SAFe principles to real-world challenges
- Foster collaboration and teamwork
- Deliver value and drive business success

Congratulations on taking the first step towards SAFe Scrum Master certification!

May your Agile journey be filled with success, growth, and meaningful contributions.

Important Note

Please be aware that the practice questions and explanations provided in "SAFe Scrum Master Exam Companion: Q&A with Explanations" are for illustrative and educational purposes only. They may not exactly replicate the actual questions or format of the SAFe Scrum Master (SSM) certification exam administered by Scaled Agile, Inc.

The primary goal of this book is to familiarize you with the question format, provide practical examples, and help you apply your knowledge of SAFe principles, Scrum frameworks, and Agile methodologies. To ensure thorough preparation for the exam, please refer to the official Scaled Agile, Inc. resources, study materials, and guidelines.

By using this book in conjunction with official Scaled Agile, Inc. study materials, including the SAFe Framework, SAFe Scrum Master course materials, and the SAFe Scrum Master exam guide, you'll be well-equipped to tackle the exam with confidence and achieve your certification goals.

NOTE ON CONTENT

We sincerely apologize if you encounter any unintentional repetition of questions within "SAFe Scrum Master Exam Companion: Q&A with Explanations". Please be assured that any instances of repeated questions were not deliberate.

Our goal is to provide you with a comprehensive and diverse range of questions to enhance your learning experience and support your preparation for the SAFe Scrum Master (SSM) certification exam.

If you do come across any repeated questions, we kindly request your understanding and indulgence. We strive to deliver unique and valuable content to aid in your understanding of SAFe principles, Scrum frameworks, and Agile methodologies.

Your learning experience is our top priority, and we're committed to supporting you on your journey to certification success.

Thank you for choosing "SAFe Scrum Master Exam Companion"